the RSA

Typing and Word Processing Book

Margaret Rees-Boughton

RSA

EXAMINATIONS BOARD

HEINEMANN
EDUCATIONAL

Heinemann Educational Publishers,
Halley Court, Jordan Hill, Oxford OX2 8EJ
a division of Reed Educational & Professional Publishing Ltd.

MELBOURNE   AUCKLAND
FLORENCE   PRAGUE   MADRID   ATHENS
SINGAPORE   TOKYO   SAOPAULO
CHICAGO   PORTSMOUTH (NH)   MEXICO
IBADAN   GABORONE   JOHANNESBURG
KAMPALA   NAIROBI

First Published 1993
98 97 96
6 5 4 3

Company limited by guarantee in England: Registered 2161813.
Registered charity: number 327546.
Registered office: Westwood Way, Coventry, CV4 8HS.

A catalogue record for this book is available
from the British Library on request.

ISBN 0 435 45210 X

Designed and typeset by Artistix,
Adwell, Tetsworth, Oxon OX9 7DH

Produced by Mandarin Offset
Printed in Hong Kong

CONTENTS

CONTENTS

This book is for anyone who wants to acquire the knowledge and skills for office-standard text processing, whether they wish to take a qualification or not. It is, however, particularly suitable for anyone intending to take RSA examinations or National Vocational Qualifications (NVQs) in Business Administration. The RSA Typewriting Skills and Word Processing Stages II and III exams provide direct evidence for NVQs at Levels 2 and 3, assessing to the same level of occupational competence as NVQs. In their own right, these exams are recognised by employers as the qualifications which are most likely to equip a typist or word processor operator for the demands of the workplace.

The book may be used equally successfully by people learning at college or school, at home on a self-study or open learning programme, or at work.

RSA text processing exam schemes are constantly under review to ensure that they are relevant to the world of work. Qualifications, such as General NVQs and GCSE-equivalent schemes, are being developed. Whatever changes take place, however, and whatever way office technology develops, the basic knowledge and skills which this book helps learners to acquire will not alter.

A Tutor's Resource Pack, accompanying this book, is also available. An audio cassette is included in the Tutor's Resource Pack containing dictation exercises.

 When this symbol is used it will indicate that dictation is linked to the passage.

ACKNOWLEDGEMENTS

Once again, RSA Examinations Board wants to thank Margaret Rees-Boughton for researching and writing this book.

Margaret, in turn, acknowledges the contribution made by Elayne Henderson of Solihull College of Technology and students of the college for helping to field-test much of the material; and the following RSA Chief Examiners and Moderators who helped in the preparation of the assignments: Phillip Arnold, Lesley Dakin, Sue Fox, Tessa Greig, Sue North, Margaret Reid, Gill Stoker and Beryl Whittick. To all of these people Margaret and RSA here express their gratitude.

INDEX

INTRODUCTION

Lots of people use a keyboard, if only occasionally. You may be wondering whether you really need keyboard skills – it's easy just to muddle along. But in the long run it's much easier to use a keyboard properly. You'll save time and energy – and this is especially important when you're under pressure at work.

Added value

This book provides practice in office-type tasks similar to those in these RSA exams:

▶ Core Text Processing Skills

▶ Stage I Typewriting Skills and Stage I Word Processing

▶ Stage II Typewriting Skills and Stage II Word Processing.

How the book works

The Keyboard	The keyboard and simple letter and memo layouts.
Section 1	Gives you the chance to work on office-type jobs.
Section 2	Here you can work on more complex documents, including tables.
Section 3	Assignments which use all your typing skills and which may require you to compose letters and memos of your own.

Dictionary

Keep yours handy. You'll need it for each section.

All through the book, you can complete the drills, practice and workouts using either a typewriter or a word processor.

Work which is marked SAVE IT is required again for other work which comes later in the book. To help you find it again easily, include either the Working Session number or the book page number in your index.

Despite the high level of sales, on inspection we occasionally find faults which could be expected to deter buyers. The customers may buy because of the low prices, but if quality is low they will not come back.

While speaking today in London, the Chairman announced this year's figures. These results include profits from the company's newest products.

Small companies do not attend. However, large companies are usually represented at EC conferences.

Mr Alsi Kani, proprietor of Torkai Traders, has asked for improvements in terms, with discounts for bulk orders. Can we help?

Sylvia, I find it is difficult for me to submit this claim, when we have had a long, happy business relationship.

Please tell me what are the prices for these goods. I have no information. Therefore, I cannot proceed with payment.

The words which are, we feel, inappropriate are: 'confident' and 'happy', which could better be expressed as: 'reassured' and 'hopeful'.

APPENDIX

Starting from scratch?

Before you start, run a machine check to save time and give yourself confidence later on.

Machine check

Look in your manual/guide and make yourself a note of how to:

▶ switch on – and start up the system

▶ load A4 paper and envelopes

▶ set margins – and reset them for a shorter or longer line

▶ move to a new line, and leave lines clear

▶ find your exact place (using the cursor on a screen, or moving to the printing point on a typewriter)

▶ make corrections

▶ save and print work with a word processor.

4. Punctuate sensibly

Type these sentences, adding or changing punctuation marks to make meaning more easily understood:

Despite the high level of sales on inspection we occasionally find faults which could be expected to deter buyers, the customers may buy because of the low prices but if quality is low they will not come back.

While speaking today in London the Chairman announced this years figures, these results include profits from the companys newest products.

Small companies do not attend. However large companies are usually represented at EC conferences.

Mr Alsi Kani proprietor of Torkai Traders has asked for improvements in terms with discounts for bulk orders, can we help?

Sylvia I find it is difficult for me to submit this claim when we have had a long happy business relationship.

Please tell me what are the prices for these goods? I have no information, therefore, I cannot proceed with payment.

The words which are we feel inappropriate are confident and happy which could better be expressed as reassured and hopeful.

Compare your answers with those on the next page.

After completing this section you should be able to:

▶ use the keyboard fluently

▶ type simple memos and letters.

Before you start

▶ Master the machine check points on page 2.

▶ Find your dictionary and keep it with you as you work.

The keyboard

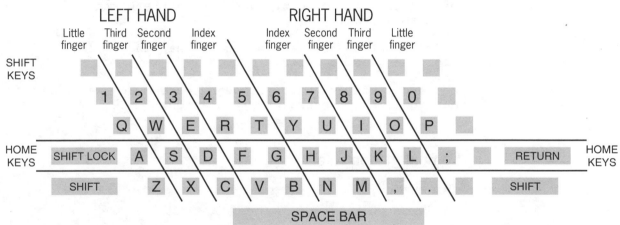

Home keys

The middle row of alphabet keys (**a, s, d, f, j, k, l, ;**) is your base line. It's often called the home row.

The base line or home row is where you position your fingers while not typing. After using a key on another row, you should immediately bring the typing finger back to join your other fingers at the base line.

Use one of your thumbs to tap the space bar.

Basing your keys on the home row helps you to learn to type the alphabet keys without looking at the keyboard.

This book has keyboard drills which include the figure keys. These are to help you find the figures easily, but unless you type figures very often, you may prefer not to touch-type numbers.

NB: you won't spot this type of error unless you read paragraphs 'aloud' to yourself, so that you can 'hear' what is typed.

If any of the above examples are not immediately clear to you, ask someone to help.

- facts which are easily checked, such as dates, names, prices
- words for which you always *wonder* about the right spelling – look them up and be sure
- missing punctuation marks, such as:

```
How much will the fares cost.  It is important to know at
this stage.

The book is called "The Tide Will Turn, and we believe it
costs £14.99.

The company - Jones, Japes and Mankin will not be able to
resist the take-over bid without your support.


We shall, therefore rely on you to cast your votes
promptly.
```

- repeated words, such as:

```
The matter will be be brought before the Board on
on Tuesday next.

We shall not be able to to see Mr Chassington before
before he goes to Paris.

The report stated that, although the company was solvent,
that the risk of bankruptcy was strong.
```

The final golden rule:
- check facts
- scan
- read with attention, 'saying' it to yourself.

```
        3   4   5   6
          E   R   T   Y
SHIFT LOCK    D   F   G   H                    RETURN
  SHIFT         C   V   B   N                    SHIFT
            SPACE BAR
```

Space bar and return key
Use your thumb for space bar, and little finger for return key.

Don't clench your fist or your arm will ache.

Workout 1
TYPE Five times: r t f g v b (return)

Try to keep your little finger over the **a** whilst you are moving your first finger out from **f** and back again.

Workout 2
TYPE Five times: f r f t f g f v f b f (return)

Shift lock
Press shift lock for capitals. Remember to release it for next line.

Workout 3
TYPE F T F R F G F V F B F T F (return)
      f t f r f g f v f b f t f (return)
      F T F R F G F V F B F T F

Try to type these lines accurately, without stopping and without looking at the keys while you type:

TYPE f r f t f g f v f b f (return)
      F V F G F R F T F B F (return)
      f f r r f f g g f b f (return)
      f f f r r r g g g b f (return)
      F F V F R F G F R T F (return)
      f r t g f v b g f v f (return)

Check
Did you type all of the above exercises accurately including spaces and capitals?

If so, move on to Working Session 2.

Made mistakes?
Type each line again until you're confident it's right. Have another go at the whole of the exercise in which that line appears. When it's accurate, go on to Working Session 2.

LEFT HAND · FIRST FINGER

THE KEYBOARD

WORKING SESSION 1

3. Spotting errors
(See also Proofreading procedures Section Two).

Golden rule: Use your Spellchecker first. Then read.

Watch specially for:
- pairs of letters incomplete
  within a word, such as:

```
beter necesary acomodate discusion remited
```

ending and starting words, such as:

```
we shall eave,  the nding,  far eaching,  but hen,
we nclose, car epairs,
```

- words/hyphens repeated at beginning of line, such as:

```
We start from the assumption that we cannot go any
any further.
```

```
It is important to realise how much effort is expen-
-ded on these matters.
```

- words not completed at beginning of line, such as:

```
We shall never be able to thank you enough for hav-
us to stay with you.
```

```
What was the result of the investigation into finan
at the plant?
```

- real words used wrongly
  right sound, wrong spelling, such as:

```
There are know doubts about it now.
```

```
We cannot tell if there company is profitable.
```

nearly the right sound, wrong spelling, such as:

```
If we are not careful we shall loose the business.
We have asked the Chairman to advice us.
There are a lot off people coming to the meeting.
We hope it gets of to a good start.
```

NB: if you *pronounce* words correctly, you're more likely to spell them correctly. Your dictionary will help.

- wrong word but a real one, such as:

```
We shall not be able to go to the meeting (instead of
We shall now be able to go to the meeting)
```

```
The junior staff are not excepted to work overtime.
```

```
Senior staff will not be effected by the change in hours.
```

APPENDIX

```
   5   6   7   8
    T   Y   U   I

SHIFT LOCK      G   H   J   K        RETURN

   SHIFT        B   N   M   ,        SHIFT

              SPACE BAR
```

Home keys

Use the middle row of keys: **a s d f   j k l ;** as your baseline. Start with your fingers over this row and reach up and down to others.

Reach out with your first finger and bring it back to **j** each time.

Workout 4

TYPE   Five times: j u j m j y j n j m j (return)

Return key

Practise stretching **your little finger** to Return. If you move your whole hand, you'll waste time getting fingers back into position over 'home' keys.

Workout 5

TYPE   j h j n j m j h j y j u m j (return) (shift lock on)
       J H J N J M J H J Y J U M J (return) (shift lock off)
       j h j n j m j h j y j u m j (return)

Now you can watch out for capitals and get your shift lock on.

TYPE   JU JH JN JM JU JY JH JM JU JH JN JY (return)
       ju jh jn jm ju jy jh jm ju jh jn jy (return)

Bring your finger back to **j** before typing **h**.

juh juy jhy jhu jhn jhm jmn jyn jym jyh (return)

Try to type these lines accurately, without stopping and without looking at the keys while you type:

TYPE   j u j y j h j m j n j (return)
       J M J H J U J Y J N J (return)
       juj jhj jyj jnj jmj (return)

Check

No mistakes? Even all spacing and capitals OK? Good – go on to Working Session 3.

Made mistakes?

Type each line again until you're confident it's right. Have another go at the whole of the exercise in which that line appears. When it's accurate, go on to Working Session 3.

RIGHT HAND • FIRST FINGER

WORKING SESSION 2

THE KEYBOARD

2. Drills for correcting spellings and common letter sequences

-able	manageable suitable mailable untraceable uncomfortable serviceable advisable replaceable changeable available
age	manage shortage carriage garage discouraged postage pilferage disengage engagements page agendas agency
-ence	difference sequence absence influence independence competence reference confidence intelligence presence
-ly	lovely sincerely likely lately truly busily fully
-ance	assurance insurance distance romance dance guidance entrance relevance importance brilliance resistance
-ible	irresistible indefensible responsible plausible legible visible feasible admissible audible accessible credible
ch	church research chemicals cheque check Chicago chance children chief china chocolate China Chester choice
th	three thirty their there thanks although nothing through rather think thought anything everything
dis-	discussion disappoint disadvantage disagree disapprove disasters discharged disclosed discipline discotheques
mis-	misadventure misapprehend misguided mistaken misgiving miscellaneous mischief misconduct miserable misfortune
-ing	changing managing engaging judging disparaging waging chancing menacing entrancing dancing facing enhancing
tr	trying trusting struggling trade distributes strength attributes distrust industrial destructive instructed
-ary	dictionary secondary plenary tertiary contrary actuary diary salary domicillary literary monetary ordinary
con	consider disconcerted condition concurrent consecutive uncontrolled congregation conclusion contract conclude
com	communities computer composed accommodation complaints committee computation recommend complied complications
-tion	action mention dictionary affection depreciation potion cautionary sections destruction instructions stationery
ment	mention increment payment treatment detriment ailment moment mentor disappointments puzzlement bewilderment
ph	photography physics phantom hyphen telephoned paragraphs pharmacy phenomenon Philadelphia philosophy phraseology
ter	laughter territory terrain daughter disaster terminate terminology stern terminus terrible terrace terse term

	E	R	T	Y	U	I		
SHIFT LOCK		D	F	G	H	J	K		RETURN
SHIFT		C	V	B	N	M	,		SHIFT

SPACE BAR

Workout 6

TYPE frf ftf fgh fvf fbv juj jyj jhj jmj jnj hgh fjf jfj
fry tub jut hug fug mug hut fur nut nutty
huffy thumb grubby fury tubby gummy numb
ruff funny butty rum rummy hymn

Shift key

Hold down **left** shift key, using your little finger, while you type a
letter with your right hand.

Workout 7

> Don't waste time using the shift lock for only one capital.

TYPE
```
Mr Hugh Jutt
Mr J H Yungh
```

Hold down **right** shift key, using your little finger, while you type a
letter with your left hand.

TYPE
```
Burt Trygh
Guy Vynth
```

Check

Use the chart at top of this page to see which hand will type, so
which shift key to use. Try not to look at the keyboard while you type.

Workout 8 (Type all these names at the left margin.)

TYPE
```
Mr Grumb            Mr Hugh Gruvy
Mr J Vynt           Mr V Bunty
Bunty Trubb         Gryff Hynt
```

Practise what you've learned

Try to type these lines accurately, without stopping and without
looking at the keys while you type:

TYPE
```
Mr Gumm try gym Mr Hugh Grufty gym
Mr J Vynt tub fun Mr Hugh Grumb grunt
Mr V Bunty numb nub hub grub gruff
```

Accurate?

You're ready for Working Session 4.

Made mistakes?

Practise again line by line, then try the whole exercise again.
When it's right, you're ready for Working Session 4.

THE KEYBOARD

TWO HANDS

WORKING SESSION 3

R   Rere & Rarly are responsible for repairing or restoring the rear areas of our residence.

S   Some say she still is suspicious of simple statements issued by several statesmen and senators.

T   A test of truth is timely. Ten attestors took the oath to tell the truth, the whole truth and nothing but the truth.

U   Your uncle undertook a journey on an urban bus route to Universal Studios.

V   Vivian revived Vince who eventually ventured into the elevator to travel down to the vestibule.

W   The wide windows were wasted in the west wing where the view was not worthwhile.

X   Six extra exams are expected and exemptions will be extended.

Y   Young & Company employ young people to make trays in the factory at Bray Yard.

Z   The zoo staff were puzzled by the size of the gazebo.

Select the drill for the **figure** which catches you out and type it three times without stopping.

1   Use 111 bricks to make 11 piles of 11 and then another 11.

2   Her address is 222 Staveley Road, London W2 22XS.

3   Our order is for 33 buckets reference 31323.

4   We leave on 4 May at 4 pm and arrive at 4 am 4 days later.

5   Please send 55 copies to 55 Gretry Road, Bristol BR55 5TT.

6   He has 666 books on 6 shelves and in 66 boxes 6" deep.

7   We send Order 771727 dated 7/7 for 717 items of 7 types.

8   87654321, 87654321, 87654321, 887766, 88817888, 18283848.

9   Number 99 prefixes all new items: 991, 992, 993, 994, 995.

0   1234567890, 10, 20, 30, 40, 50, 60, 70, 80, 90, 100, 1000.

```
      2   3   4
        W   E   R
SHIFT LOCK  S   D   F              RETURN
   SHIFT      X   C   V            SHIFT
              SPACE BAR
```

Workout 9

TYPE Five times: d e d c d e d c d e d c d

Stretch your finger up from **d** to **e**. Bring it back over **d** and tuck
down to **c**. Don't bounce your hand.

Workout 10

TYPE
```
deed cede deed cede deed cede deer reed reedy fed feed
tree deft ever bred heed gent free rent freed ten tent
```

Remember to keep your hand straight from knuckles to wrist.
First finger stays over **f** even while typing with second finger.

Relax your
shoulders and
upper arms.

TYPE
```
freed breed deter greed green every creed greet edged
deterred December edged verger refer referred fretted
```

Try to type the following lines without stopping. Try not to look at
the keys while typing:

TYPE berth Betty here jeered jetty need demur
turned gummed burned herd every ever
the there three thud they theft them
dry hug hugged turfed hummed muddy
thumb cry hemmed deem deemed here
Herbert hugged Gert but jeered Greg
Fred Edger greeted them by Derby but
then they burned the Rugby fern

Check

Did you type all of the above exercises accurately including all
spacing?

You're ready for Working Session 5.

Made mistakes?

Type again each wrong line. Then try the whole exercise in which
the line(s) appear. When it's right, you're ready for Working
Session 5.

THE KEYBOARD

WORKING SESSION 4

1. Keying errors

Select the drill for the **letter** which catches you out!

A   Anna and Ada are in the airport area and are attending a party at Amman Arena Annexe.

B   Bill, Barbara, Beryl, Bobby and Brendan belong to Babbington Bowls Club, Berkshire.

C   The company chairman is confident the Consolidated Coconut & Chocolate Company can convert its currency deficit.

D   Dividends are decidedly reduced due to declining demand in the divisions dedicated to diamonds.

E   Every employee is entitled to receive a leaflet explaining the elements of competence expected.

F   The Fraud Office found no fault which affected efficiency in the fulfilment of fiscal and financial affairs.

G   Gregory & Grange run a garage in Grangemouth and the manager is Graham Garrington.

H   Hight Haulage Ltd have had heavy haulage charges which have hampered and hindered them this month.

I   Interim results in the insurance industry indicate improved activities and profits in the business.

J   Jemma Jayne Jenks joined the showjumping team in January and is daughter of Judge John Jenks.

K   Katy works in the kitchens at the bakery and takes cakes to Kirsty at the bank in Kettering.

L   Lily sang a lilting melody when lying on a lilo at Little Lulworth while Lester looked longingly at the lemonade.

M   My most memorable moments made mighty impressions, which may or may not be momentous.

N   News editors need news nightly and can never understand anybody not wanting to know.

O   You ought to overlook poor origins and open your doors to those who obviously ought to come in.

P   Piebald pigeons with patches are plentiful in Poppingham. People pay to peer at them pecking.

Q   Questy & Co acquired a quantity of high quality quarters in The Quadrant, a quiet area in the Basque town of Quadre.

```
  2 3 4 5 6 7 8
   W E R T Y U I
SHIFT LOCK   S D F G H J K        RETURN
  SHIFT      X C V B N M ,        SHIFT
           SPACE BAR
```

Workout 11

Try to type the following without looking at the keys:

> **Don't get too tired. Take a short rest at the end of each line.**

TYPE *tender meter Brent Derby Rugby deterred metered demented ended creed decree breech cheered chugged grunt greeted brunch crunch needed freed referred referenced mend grunted*

Check

No mistakes?
Good – on to Workout 12.

Need to try again?
Type again the words in which you made mistakes, then have another go at the line(s) in which they appear.

Time check

You have five minutes to type Workout 12 without mistakes.

Workout 12

Start each new item at your left margin.

TYPE
```
Fred Henty ceded free rent every December
Bert met Betty Hunt there even then
Netty trudged there but then jeered Greg

Mr Greg Hute
Rugby

Mr Bert Unver
Brent

June Fentugh
Bury

Mr Brent tendered the judgement
Betty burned her reference
Never defend the brute under the fence
Feed the runner by the trench
```

> **Press return twice to leave clear space between items.**

Check

When you can type Workout 12 without mistakes in five minutes you are ready to start work on figures.

THE KEYBOARD

WORKING SESSION 5

Drew Davidson
Editorial Director
Mondori Publishing Inc
1012 Park Avenue South
New York
NY 1015

Sec: change The World of the Greeks to The Greek World throughout

Dear Drew   (sec: state days)   (state month)
I'm writing to confirm that I will def. be in the States from 12 to 13 of [next month].

——————————— HOLLYWOOD LIVES

As you know I particularly want to discuss our co-promotional plans for Hollywood Lives, so it would be useful if Marjorie Wentworth and Roger Farley from Publicity could be involved in our meeting at some point.

THE WORLD OF THE GREEKS
On another subject, thank you for yr fax of yesterday about the World of the Greeks re the proposed new paperback edition of The World of the Greeks. //I'm afraid I've (NP) failed to clarify the costs on this book adequately.

The total projected sales forecast is 17,000 not 15,000 which makes the gross profit margin 71%. I enclose the estimate for yr. info. //The hardback edition of The (NP) World of the Greeks is now out of stock in the UK and we do not plan to reprint. We therefore hope to publish the paperback by the end of [see: 2 months' time]. Yr stock w/ arrive shortly after. Pls forward any special shipping instructions asap.

Best wishes
Yours sncly
Perminder Rahima
Editorial Director

I've finally managed to pin down Adam Arnelli of the Phoenix Press to a meeting on the 5th. Could I arrange to spend the following day with you?

Sec: write memo to Jim Dexter in Finance to arrange currency $150 cash, $800 travellers cheques. I'd like it a couple of days before I fly + I don't want to come in at the weekend to pick it up!

```
2  3  4  5  6  7  8
W   E   R   T   Y   U   I
SHIFT LOCK    S   D   F   G   H   J   K          RETURN
SHIFT        X   C   V   B   N   M   ,          SHIFT
                    SPACE BAR
```

Workout 13

TYPE Five times: `de3 fr4 ft5 jy6 ju7`

If you let your hand 'bounce' up to the figures you'll waste time getting your fingers back to the home keys, ready to find the next letters.

Workout 14

Leave two spaces to separate different items on same line.

Keep your arms as still as possible.

Tap two spaces to separate items on a line.

TYPE
```
The 3 met Greg there
then 4 greeted Gert
The 5 deer turned here but 6 hugged the edge
They met 36 red but 7 grey deer
Bert freed 367 by 6
Reference 37445   Term 4   Meter 6673   4 June
37 The Hyde  Hedgebury  Rugby  CV37 6BM
```

It's particularly important to proofread for mistakes in figures. Whoever reads your work may have no way of spotting an error. You may prefer not to touch-type figures – it's better to look and to get them right.

Workout 15

TYPE
```
Mr Greg Bunter
33 Hunter Rd
DERBY
DE23 3FV

Dr V Hendry
34 Trent Cr
RUGBY
CV35 4JD
```

Check

No mistakes?

When you can type Workouts 14 and 15 accurately, you're ready to move on to more figure work.

STRETCH UP TO THE FIGURES

THE KEYBOARD

Assignment 5

In the last of this series of assignments for Mondori Publishing you are to type a financial estimate table – use your paper horizontally or adapt layout to suit paper with shorter edge at the top. There is a letter from the editorial director, Perminder Rahima, which also requires you to compose your own memo to Finance.

Handwritten notes:

1st & 2nd print

New Book/Reprint Estimate
Title: The Greek World — Caps
Price: £3.95
Estimate Sale per year: 4000

Print Numbers	4000 (1st year)	17 000 (Lifetime)
Unit Cost	0.525	0.512
Revenue UK	4953.20	40%	5474.00	40%
Revenue US	7429.80	60%	21 898.80	60%
Total Revenue	12 383.00	100%	32 848.20	100%

Sec – leave space, about .25mm/1"

Product fixed	1916	15.50%	1916	3.5%
Print Binding Paper	2100	17.0%	8705	15.9%
Total Production	4116	33.2%	10621 5376	19.4%
Royalty	1238	10.0%	5475 ✓	10.0%
Gross Margin	7029 £8288	59%	38652	71.0%

Check your keyboard. If yours is the same as the diagram above, use the shift key to type the symbols shown over the figures.

If your keyboard is different, use the chart on page 3 to check:
• which fingers to use
• whether the symbols need the shift key.

Workout 16

TYPE

Church hymns 33/56/734/67
Ref 463/55 then Ref 6675 @ £56
Herbert & Jerry   37 Berry Rd   Bury
Bench reference 3637 @ £45
Ferry & Henty   3 Church Rd Derby

> **Remember:** you can use two spaces to separate items on a line.

Check

Remember how important it is to double check figures to make sure you've made no mistakes.

Accurate?

Including all figures and symbols? Good – move on to Workout 17.

Made mistakes?

You may prefer not to touch-type figures and symbols. Don't move on till you're sure you can get them right.

Workout 17

TYPE

```
Henry Bryce & Hythe
     34/38 Dent Rd
         Myner Green
             FRENCH CENTRE
```

> This spacing style, where each line is moved to the right under the line above, is known as 'indenting'.

When you're confident you have mastered these keys, move on to Working Session 8, where you can check your progress so far.

Specification Sheet : Long Twin-incision Skirt (style 231 08 9X)

See: Rule it up like this ple.

Colour : Black
Size : 12

See: leave space for sketch about 1"/25mm before top rule of table.

Name/Ref. no.	Amount per garment	Price	Price per garment
Wool gabardine 0135	3·2 m	£1·72 p/m	£5·50
4144D	18 cm	£0·85	£0·85
Brass 834Y	3	£0·80	£2·40
Nylon 1089	3·2 m / 58 cm	£0·58 p/m	£1·86
K11178 Audrey Lambert Jean Mitchell ①		£0·50 p/m	£0·29
		£3·50	£3·50
		/	/
		/	/
M836	12 m	£0·36 p/m	£0·11
/	/	/	£14·51

Fabric
Zip
Button
Lining
Interlining
Embroidery
Pleating
Boning
Thread
Total per garment

Check yourself

Workout 18

Can you type the following without:

- a keyboard chart
- looking at the keys?

TYPE
```
Mr Fred Edge
Rugby

Dr Bert Unver
Brent

June Fentugh
Bury

Judge Brent rendered the judgement
Berty Hedger burned her reference
Never defend the brute under the fence
Feed the runner by the trench
```

> Remember: tap 'return' twice to leave a clear line.

Accurate?

Good! Move on to Workout 19.

Made mistakes?

Try again. When you can get it right, move on.

Timing

Workout 19

Try to type the following accurately within one minute:

TYPE
```
The judge greeted the men then rendered the judgement
Greg never fed the runner by the hedge
He turned by the church
```

Check

If you finished in one minute, you are typing at about 20 words a minute.

If you weren't able to finish in time, try again but don't rush and make mistakes.

Accurate?

You are making excellent progress. Move on to Working Session 9.

Made mistakes?

Have another try. If necessary, slow down in order to get it right before moving on.

THE KEYBOARD

WORKING SESSION 8

MEMO

From: Vivien Peters (Designer)

To:
- Vivek Khatkar (Production Manager)
- Rose Alphouse (Marketing Manager)
- Robert Meecham (Sales Manager)
- Karen Dallas (Director)
- Stephen North (Director)
- Kathy Miles (In-house Model)

Subject: <u>In-house Design Meeting</u>.

I wd. like to arrange an in-house ~~design meeting~~ feedback session on the garment designs wh. I have been in formulation since our last meeting in December.

We have 15 styles to show you, inc. the new swimwear and trouser ranges.

I wd. like these garments to be given yr. imm. attention as I intend them to be included in our final Summer collection and to be seen in our ~~forthcoming~~ series of fashion shows.

The meeting will take place in the showroom and I suggest a date of 15 of [next month] at 1.30pm. Please fill in the form below and return ~~before~~ lunchtime on Friday of next week (sec. give date)

Q W E

SHIFT LOCK | A S D | RETURN

SHIFT | Z X C | SHIFT

SPACE BAR

Get the feel of the keys into the third finger.

Workout 20

TYPE Five times: s w s w s x s

Close your eyes and type the letters **s w x** and the figure **2**.

Repeat until you can type them at least once accurately with your eyes closed.

TYPE sew sews wed weds dew dews sum sums dress dresses
sex sexes Eve vex vexes crew crews web webs seven
West End Essex Webb Webster Street Guest Crescent

Workout 21

Remember, it's not good to 'bounce' your hand.

TYPE There were 22 mugs 23 huts 23 shrubs
24 bushes 26 swedes
Just 2 trenches were dug here
We were there when 23 cubs were runners
The rents must be sent by 23rd December when the new judges meet
There were few streets where we were met
22 crew members were there

Workout 22
Here is extra practice for the third finger. See how many times you can type these accurately in 5 minutes.

TYPE Start each line at left margin

The men met at 22 Wessex Street but there were 32 guests when they were greeted by Fred 'Return' twice to show new para
Mrs Best judged the best 4 dresses were the 2 by Eve and the 2 by Jess
When there were 234 here we sent 25

Check
Be confident it's right before moving on to Working Session 10.

Day 5   7 April
09.00:   Dai Ichi
11.00:   Kaken Clothes
15.00:   Sankyo
HOTEL: Palace Hotel

Days 6-9   8-11 April

Yamamoti Fashion Fair ⟵ (spaced caps centre)
   HOTEL: Palace Hotel

Day 10   12 April

FLIGHT: VS 901 Tokyo - London
DEPART: 12.30   Tokyo
ARRIVE: 16.45   London Heathrow

(Secretary: write letter to confirm bookings with Palace Hotel. Remember to tell them they'll be 3 extra people on 7-11 April (see Karen Dallas's memo in section 1, Assignment 5 for their names.)

Workout 23

TYPE Five times: `exert Essex vexed Sussex next text textures`

Tuck your elbow into your side. If you twist your arm to get to the top row, you'll make your shoulder ache.

Workout 24

TYPE
```
West & Webster
237 Hendry Street
Esher
Surrey


Hunter & Hester
425 Green Street
Shrewsbury


Mr Greg Brunster
24 The Hyde
DERBY
DE23   7VB


Mrs Jenny Fentry
327 Crumen Street
RUGBY
CV26   2GN
```

This style for addresses, where all the lines start at the same point, is called 'Block'.

Check

Names must always be right. People can be offended if their names are mis-spelled.

The right and full address is essential to avoid postal delay. What's missing from the first two addresses? Always ask for the post code when noting addresses.

Timing

Workout 25

Aim to type the following within one minute:

TYPE
```
fry grub vest dust judge fender must there crumb buy
We went there yet the 22 dresses were then sent here
```

Check

If you completed the two lines accurately within one minute – and didn't have to look at the keys – you're already using half the keyboard and typing at approximately 20 words a minute.

Assignment 4

In the final group of assignments for Escadia, Vivien Peters is arranging an in-house design meeting. There is a specification table. Either use your paper horizontally for this, or with the short edge at the top (in which case you may have to divide lines). You also have to type up the itinerary for Karen Dallas's trip to Japan and compose your own letter confirming a hotel booking.

ITINERARY

for the trip to Japan of
KAREN DALLAS/ STEPHEN NORTH

Day 1   3 April

FLIGHT: VS 900   London Heathrow – Tokyo
DEPART: 14.00   Tokyo (next day)
ARRIVE: 10.00   London Heathrow
HOTEL: Palace Hotel
          Marunouchi
          1-1-1 Chiyoda Ku
          Tokyo

Day 2   4 April

FLIGHT: JL 119 Tokyo – Osaka
DEPART: 16.10 Tokyo
ARRIVE: 17.10 Osaka
HOTEL: Osaka Grand Hotel
          Nakanoshima
          2-3-18 Kuta Ka
          Osaka

Day 3   5 April

10.00:   Ono Fashions
14.00:   Sumitomo Fashion Group
FLIGHT: Osaka – Tokyo
DEPART: 20.00 Osaka
ARRIVE: 21.00 Tokyo
HOTEL: Palace Hotel

Day 4   6 April

REST DAY

1 2 3
Q W E
SHIFT LOCK   A S D
SHIFT   Z X C   RETURN
SHIFT
SPACE BAR

Get the 'feel' of the letters.

TYPE Five times: a q a z a q l q a z a q l q
      a z a q l q a z a z a q l q

The big stretch

It will be difficult to keep your hand over the home keys while you make the big stretch to type **q** and **1**. Try not to clench your fist; avoid bouncing your hand.

Workout 26

TYPE afar add Dad as sad sash axe axed adze as ash ashes
      added washed mashed hashed gash trash shades shaded

Take time out

Your little finger may well be stiff, and your wrist may ache when you first practise these letters. Rest for a second or two at the end of each line.

Workout 27

TYPE charters squashed aqua quest acute queer query squeam
      treasures gardeners sweaters measurements breathers
      craters squares drummers barbecues sweetmeats hearsay
      dreamers trays crashed stranded exactness hastened
      swears dreamed artery ascend addendum amendment caster

      azure grazed raze amazed maze freeze freezer breeze
      breezed squeeze squat squatted squatter quay quartz
      quad quaff quadrate quantum quarender quarry quarts
      queen quasar quench zebra zanja zany zed Zen enzyme
      Zeus zest Aztec Uzbeg zebras equated hazards Zambia
      sequestrate stanza Anzac fuzzy grazed crazy quavers

Check

Have you copied each word accurately? It's easy to mis-spell words such as 'gardeners' and 'hastened'. We don't hear these words in the way they're spelled.

Accurate?

Move to Working Session 12.

Made mistakes?

It'll save you time in the long run to spend a few minutes now making sure your fingering is accurate.

LEFT HAND • FOURTH FINGER

WORKING SESSION 11

THE KEYBOARD

Complete Reconciliation Statements and
letters for three divorce petitions. We act for
the Petitioner in each case. The full name
of the individual solicitor is TREVE JAMES
DOCKER.   We type this (on the Rec. Statement)
in capitals, all underlined.

Case No 1992 (D) 1007

JOHN SMITH and ANN SMITH and DAVID JONES
                                (Co.R-)

No. —— 1009

WAYNE CHILDI and JANI LEE CHILDI (No C-R)

No.   1017

ROSY LISBETTE FRANCINE and JONTY FRANCINE
                        and CARMEL BRAGER

All 3 letters to send   1. Divorce Petition in triplicate
                        2. Marriage certificate
                        3. Reconciliation Statement
                        4. Cheque for £40.

Using a word processor

- Start with cursor at left margin as normal.
- Type first line of the first column.
- Press tab key (often marked but check your keyboard/machine guide).
- Check: has the tab key moved your cursor far enough – will there be room to type the longest line in column 1 when you come to it? Will there also be room for three or more extra spaces after the longest line?
- If 'no' to any of the above, press tab key again and repeat the check.
- If 'yes' to all of the above, type the first line of the next column.
- Press tab key and repeat check until all the columns are in place.
- It is usually quicker to type across the page, line by line than to type from top to bottom of one column before starting at the top of the next and so on.

TYPE

Dear Aunty Ada	Dear Mrs Judger	Dear Dad
Dear Mrs Hearty	Dear Ms Streeter	Dear Mum
Dear Dr Tranter	Dear Mr Manders	Dear Fred
Dear Janet	Dear Mr Feathers	Dear Ben

Using a typewriter

- Check there are no tab stops already set. Some machines have a key/lever to clear all tab stops at once; on some other machines you need to press the tab key and the tab clear key each time the carriage stops at a set tab. Check your manual/machine guide if you are unsure and not working with a tutor/supervisor.
- Set a left margin of about one inch.
- From left margin, tap space bar for the number of characters/spaces in the longest line in column 1 plus at least another three spaces.
- Press the tab set key.
- Tap the space bar for the number of characters/spaces in the longest line in column 2 plus the same number of extra spaces you tapped after column 1.
- Press the tab set key.
- Repeat until all of the tab stops are in place.
- It is usually quicker to type across the page line by line than to type from top to bottom of one column before starting at the top of the next and so on.

TYPING IN COLUMNS

THE KEYBOARD

Our ref:

Chief Clerk
Brumpton County Court
Commercial Road
Brumpton
Notts   N12 6XXD

Dear Sirs

RE:

We enclose the following:

1

2

3

4

5

Please issue accordingly.

Yours faithfully
HARDOP BLACK, CURTING & LONDSON

  Encs

Notes on preparation of the above typed form or WP template for standard letter.

- The heading may be one or two lines.
- There may be fewer than five items, but rarely more.
- Remember, we like about ten lines left clear for signatures.
- You'll also need to have room for the date, which may be typed at the left margin between reference and address *or* towards the right margin on same line as the reference.

Word-processor uses will store this as a template.

Typewriter users will prepare for use as a printed form.

Workout 28
Use your tab stops for the columns in the following exercise:

TYPE *The garden here has*

shrubs	*trees*	*bushes*
tubs	*hedges*	*grasses*
standards	*dwarfs*	*seeds*

Check
Did you leave enough room to type 'standards'? Did you leave space after that before the next column?

Revision
Leaving space helps people to read and understand documents. We use it in tables and to indicate paragraphs.

A very important part of text processing is choosing the right space.

Workout 29
Type the following short paragraphs:

Leave one clear linespace to show start of each new paragraph.

TYPE *We are wanted at the street entrance and we need Betty there when we see the members*

The nurses were seen at the ward entrance and they gave Mrs West case number 22

Mr Gray wrenched the hammer away and extracted the studs when he went

She stayed at number 11 and we were at number 12 in the same street

Check
Make sure you're using linespacing to show paragraphs.

Accurate?
Move to Working Session 13.

Made mistakes?
It'll save you time in the long run, to spend a few minutes now making sure your fingering is reliable.

THE KEYBOARD

TYPING IN COLUMNS

WORKING SESSION 12

Notes for preparation of typed form or WP template for Reconciliation Statement (previous page).

The purpose of this document is to assure the Court that in cases of divorce the solicitor has, before taking the case to Court, discussed with the client the possibilities of a reconciliation. (If the client is legally-aided, that is the legal fees will be paid through a government scheme, the Reconciliation Statement is *not* provided in this way.)

Entry points on the form/template:

(1)   No of Matter: leave at least 15 spaces

               Each case is given a case number by the Court. This number is always quoted on any correspondence and on any Court documents associated with the case.

(2) (3)   The names of the Petitioner and Respondent will be centred here.

(4)   Leave sufficient clear space after the Respondent's details to enter details of any Co-Respondent when required.

               If there is a Co-Respondent, the name will be centred here. However, there is not always a Co-Respondent involved, and this heading must not then appear (nor the word 'and' above it).

(5)   The full names of the individual solicitor must be entered (say, twenty-five spaces on a typed form).

(6, 7, 8)   Entry at each of these points may be 'Petitioner' or 'Respondent'.

(9, 10, 11)   Day, month, year.

(12)   We like ten linespaces left clear for signature.

SECTION THREE

Copy the following letter and envelope. You will be using the keys we have already practised, so you can focus on layout.

Letters

See page 91 for Style Guide to Letters.

- Start at about one inch from the top edge of your A4 paper.
- Set a left margin of about two inches.
- Use a new line for each part of an address (postcodes can go with the last item).

TYPE

```
314 Westway Street
Nethertean
Derby    DE21 R31
```
'Return' twice & type date at margin   *21 January*

Leave another clear line after the date

```
Dear James

We are here at the Centre and can see Jenny next
Tuesday

Best regards
```

Envelopes

A 'DL' envelope is usually used for an A4 letter. The DL measures 110mm x 220mm – about 4½" x 8½". Leave some room for the stamp and postmark – press 'return' to leave about 15 lines clear. Use a left margin of about 25 spaces – 2" to 2½" – so that the address will be around the middle of the envelope.

Word processors

If you have a printer which will accept envelopes on single-sheet feed, you will be able to type your envelope as above.

If not, the different procedures in your office may be:

- use window envelopes (no need to address these, because the address typed on the letter will show through the window)
- type envelopes on a typewriter
- print addresses on labels, using a word processor, and stick these on envelopes
- use handwriting for envelopes.

NB: in RSA Word Processing exams, envelopes are not required.

INTRODUCING LETTERS AND ENVELOPES

THE KEYBOARD

IN THE BRUMPTON COUNTY COURT

No of Matter: _____ **(1)**

B E T W E E N :

(2)   Petitioner

and

(3)   Respondent

and

(4)   Co-Respondent

I, (5)   of Messrs HARDOP BLACK, CURTING &

LONDSON of 7/9 Victoria Road, Herslea in the County of Nottingham,

Solicitors acting on behalf of the (6)   in the above cause hereby

certify that I have discussed with the (7)   the possibility of a

reconciliation and that I have given to the (8)   the names and

addresses of persons qualified to help effect a reconciliation.

Dated this (9)   day of (10)   199(11).

(12)

Signed ....

of Hardop Black, Curting and Landson

There are notes on the next page to help you with this template.

To: The District Judge

Workout 30

TYPE Five times: `ki8ik, k i 8 i k, ki8ik,`

Practise typing the same keys with your eyes closed.

Workout 31

TYPE
```
kick kitchen Kate Katy kin skinning kitsch
skiffs skits kits kitbags kittenish knaves
skims skirmish kidney karate keener knight
```

Repeat Workout 31 twice. Type as fast as you can manage.

Take time out

After that rush, give your fingers a rest. While doing that, look up in your dictionary the meanings of any words you don't know.

Accuracy

Type Workout 31 again at your normal speed and aim for no mistakes at all.

The comma

Workout 32

TYPE
```
We were there, yet we were unaware that Katy, the nurse,
was there
Rick had his ticket, his drink and his handkerchief in
his hand
Nick, my friend, was here and he, Nick, said there were
fewer men here this year
Jim said there was, as far as he knew, insufficient
interest in getting fair, decent and safe treatment
```

(no space before typing commas)

Check

Type Workout 32 again. This time check your technique.

Elbows tucked in? Fingers hovering over home row? Straight line (not humps) from knuckles to wrists?

Good technique helps accuracy as well as saving effort.

RIGHT HAND · SECOND FINGER

THE KEYBOARD

WORKING SESSION 14

Assignment 3

The work is for:
Hardop Black, Curting & Londson
Solicitors
7/9 Victoria Road
HERSLEA
Nottinghamshire NG22 4BQ

The work is:

- templates to be created for word processing
or
- blank forms to be produced for use with typewriter
- completed items using templates/forms.

Documents:

- standard letter sending a petition to the County Court
- standard details for Reconciliation Statement.

You need:

- index and storage details for word processing
- access to photocopier to make copies later.

Workout 33

Try not to look at the keys while you type:

TYPE
```
We are sure there are things which must be handed in
It is never unfair if great men are in charge
We need every cent we can muster if we are, in the end,
wanting a fair share in the market
It was very exciting when the Manager gave us the badge
as the best team
```

Check

Managed not to look and no errors? Move on to the next Workout.

Had to look for some key(s)? Practise with those keys for a few moments until you're confident you can find them. Then move on.

Workout 34

Type the following three columns of words. Set tabs for the second and third columns (see Working Session 12).

TYPE
```
screwdriver     Tuesday         whiskered
scrutiny        Wednesday       watershed
scrubbing       Thursday        watertight
screening       Friday          warnings
sinister        Saturday        withdrawing
sweetheart      Sunday          wizardry
```

Check

In your dictionary look up the meaning of 'watershed'.
Check the meaning of any other words you didn't fully understand.

Made any typing mistakes?
Before moving on, type again the words you got wrong.

Accurate?
Good. Move on to Workout 35.

Using a typewriter?
Clear your tab stops (see Working Session 12).

Workout 35

TYPE Five times: `ki8ik, k8ik, i8ik,  ,8ik`

TYPE
```
8/8/88 and 8 March 88 and 18 January 87 and 8 August 86
1, 2, 3 and 8 are the best
I want 8 knives and 8 saucers, Mary
The 18 rugs, the 28 basins, the 38 brushes and 48 trays
There were 8 here by 8 am and 18 by 8 in the evening
Ring 821 8488 and the maid may answer
```

Check

Take time to check figures very carefully. It's better to look at the keys while typing figures than to risk a mistake.

I'm glad to hear you're coming to the Greenfingers Club next month. The chairman, Derek ~~Skelley~~ Shelley, showed me some newspaper cuttings from 1942 about local people in various wartime activities, and these include references to Bowlson men and their peacetime jobs as gardeners and grooms at "Hoxton Hall and other large house in the county". No doubt you'll find that of use.

All the very best of luck with the next stage of your enquiries and writing.

Yours sincerely

Wayne

WAYNE P JOHNSTONE
Sh— Man—

SHIFT LOCK   K L ;   RETURN

SHIFT   , .   SHIFT

SPACE BAR

Workout 36

TYPE `l o l . l o l . l o 9 o l . l o 9 o l . l o 9`

```
loll lolly doll dolly folly golly jolly Molly
trolley follies dollies trolleys lollies
look lifts lily light leads louts welly rolls
We do look like lemons.


29 Lolling Road, Lollingworth, Leamington
2292 Lode Street, Looe, Cornwall
We received 99 loads and checked them all.
We held our own in sales drives in 1991, 1992 and 1993.
9 May 1989, 19 June 1991, 29 July 1897, 9 August 1898
Our annual meeting is to be held in London on Friday,
29 August next year.
It is the custom of our other organisation to hold its
Annual General Meetings on the last day of August of each
year, whether it is a weekend or not.
```

Check

It's worth repeating yet again: numbers and dates have to be checked very carefully. Your reader may not be able to guess if a figure is right or wrong.

Made mistakes?

Using a word processor? Correct on screen before printing. Move to Workout 37.

Using a typewriter? Type again any figures or words which you mis-keyed before moving on.

Spacing after the end of a sentence

Leave a space after the full stop to make the end of a sentence. Some people prefer to leave two or three spaces, and this is reasonable. Whichever style you choose, make sure you're consistent and leave the same number of spaces every time.

RIGHT HAND · THIRD FINGER

THE KEYBOARD

WORKING SESSION 15

Letter

Mrs Carey
Howtley Cottage
Vine Lane
Buryfield
BA4 6BTH

Dear Mrs Carey

Thank you for your recent letter.

Further to our telephone conversation yesterday,
I now enclose typed copy of the family details
brought in by Jenny Bowlson, a junior gardener
with us.   I've got an appointment to see Jenny's
mother in a couple of days' time, and with
permisssxtion from her and my Managers
I hope to encourage customers to offer any
further information they can about descendants
of Thomas Harold and the antecedents of Phillip,
who was gardener's assistant at Hoxton Hall in 1888. It may
be that Phillip was a son of Thomas Harold. ̶b̶u̶t̶
Jenny tells me her uncle, who made a half-
serious attempt to record the family's history
some time ago, has since died. There were a
lot of records which he had obtained but
not filed. It may be that the family
would be prepared for you to use them.
Jenny believes her uncle was never able to
discover any details about Thomas after
the record of his birth, nor about Phillip.

It's getting intriguing, isn't it? ̶I̶'̶m̶ ̶r̶e̶a̶l̶l̶y̶
̶f̶i̶n̶d̶i̶n̶g̶ ̶a̶ ̶g̶r̶e̶a̶t̶ ̶d̶e̶a̶l̶ ̶o̶f̶ ̶i̶n̶t̶e̶r̶e̶s̶t̶ ̶i̶n̶ ̶i̶t̶ ̶m̶y̶s̶e̶l̶f̶
̶a̶n̶d̶ I'm sure the book# will be of great
interest to customers, in due course.

Workout 37

TYPE

I looked for a coat costing less than £59.99 but was unable to find one! It seems I shall have to search elsewhere.

Laura told us her holiday was lovely last year. We think we might go to the same town next year. Laura will give us the address of the landlord of the flat she leased.

If we can, we shall be at the meeting, and I believe we shall be in time to meet every guest. This will be better than last year, when we missed quite a few of them because our train was late.

Check

As well as correcting all words, check that you have left:

- one space after every comma
- one space between sentences (or more, if you choose, but always the same number)
- a clear line to separate paragraphs.

Accurate?

Move to Workout 38.

Made mistakes?

Type again the sentences in which you made mistakes. When you can get them right, move to Workout 38.

Workout 38

Set up for this Workout:

- normal left margin (about one inch)
- one tab stop (see Working Session 12) for start of the dotted lines
- double linespacing (tap 'return' twice or give 'print' instruction for word processors).

The words in the following list are very uncommon. They provide practice in:

- copying unfamiliar words
- concentration and checking – letter by letter
- using your dictionary for other than spellings.

THE KEYBOARD

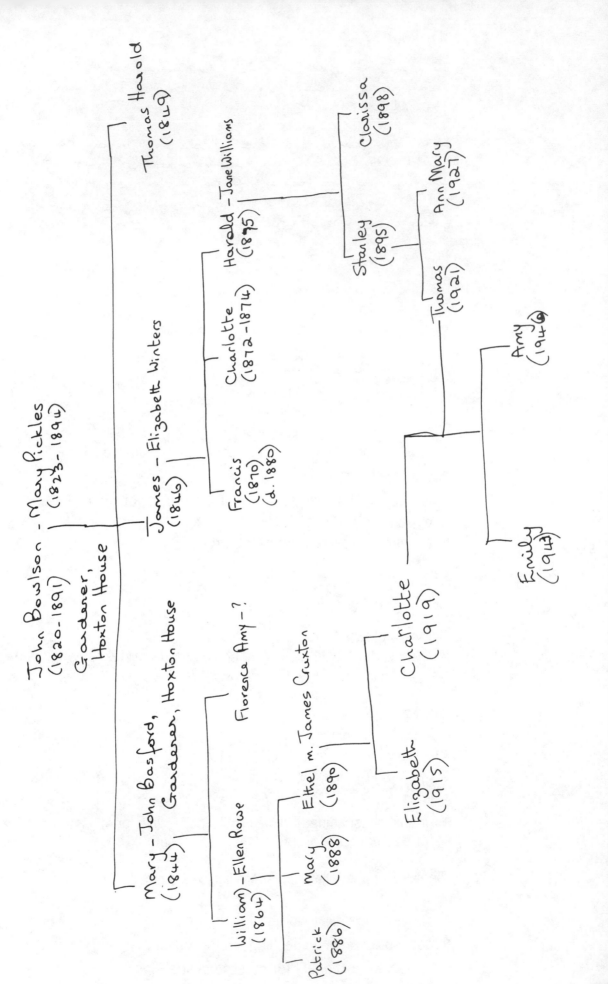

John Bowlson — Mary Pickles
(1820-1891)   (1823-1894)
Gardener,
Hoxton House

Thomas Harold
(1849)

James — Elizabeth Winters
(1846)

Charlotte
(1872-1874)

Harold — Jane Williams
(1875)

Francis
(1870)
(d. 1880)

Stanley
(1895)

Clarissa
(1898)

Thomas
(1921)

Ann Mary
(1927)

Mary — John Basford,
(1844)   Gardener, Hoxton House

William — Ellen Rowe
(1864)

Florence Amy — ?

Patrick
(1886)

Mary
(1888)

Ethel m. James Cruxton
(1890)

Elizabeth
(1915)

Charlotte
(1919)

Emily
(1947)

Amy
(1948)

ASSIGNMENT 2

Type each word, press 'tab', type dots (full stop) to line-end (about one inch from right edge of paper)

TYPE farina ....

cynicism ....

jaghir ....

faquir ....

zenith ....

mitigate ....

You will need to bring this back to screen if you're a word processor user. If you're using a typewriter you will have to use your paper copy again.

Check

Dictionaries give more than spellings. Look up the unusual words above, to find:

- how to pronounce them
- their meanings.

Revision

Workout 39

Type as quickly as you can:

TYPE As far as we can see we are safe here and when we get to Bury we may meet a trader there.

Harry and Barry are great mates and can share the burden.

Check

The aim of Workout 39 was for you to get your fingers moving as quickly as possible.

Type it again. This time try to go even faster.

Now

Type Workout 39 again, but this time at your normal speed and trying to make no mistakes.

Now you're ready to move on to Working Session 17.

WORD PRACTICE

THE KEYBOARD

Memo

Mrs Bentigou and Lisa
Wayne

NEW SERIES OF BOOKLETS

I enclose notes of our meeting three weeks ago today (type date please)
Apologies for the delay in getting these to you.

Following our meeting I contacted Mrs Carey, who had already followed up some information she had received from her own sources. The result is quite exciting.

In a visit to one of the houses featured in the earlier series, the owner had shown Mrs Carey a diary belonging to her great-grandmother, dated for 1888. In it, they found an entry about the garden with a reference to the gardener and his assistant. The assistant's name is one which is well-known locally — and indeed one of our own junior employees, Jenny, has the name Bowlson.

Jenny Bowlson has now produced the attached family tree. It was in handwriting & was a bit untidy because it was produced by Jenny's uncle some years ago when a half-serious attempt was being made to record the family's history. We've typed it up, therefore and I'm drafting a letter sending a copy to Mrs Carey.

If we have the family's permission, is it all right for me to display this in the shop with an enquiry if anyone can give any information to fill in the gaps. (any of)

I've got an appointment to see Jenny's mother in a couple of days' time & I'll get written permission before I do anything.

A draft of my letter to Mrs Carey is also attached, for your approval being despatched. (before)

WPJ

Workout 40
Type without looking at the keys:

TYPE
```
There are many, many knives in the drawers.
We are taking a variety with us.
We are attending the meeting next week.
```

Check
Accurate?
Good – now try to type it a bit faster.

Made mistakes?
Ring round the letters you mis-keyed; then practise the complete words a few times. Then have another try at the whole sentence before moving on.

Parts of a letter
The opening phrase of letters is called the **salutation**.

Workout 41

TYPE
```
Dear Madam, Dear Sir, Dear Miss Birch, Dear Sirs
Dear Sue, Dear Sidney, Dear Mr Knight
```

The closing phrase of letters is called the **complimentary closing**. Here are some examples.

Workout 42

TYPE
```
Best wishes, Sincere wishes, Best regards, Merry
Christmas, New Year Greetings
```

Timing
Workout 43
Try to type accurately in no more than two minutes:

TYPE
```
Dear Mr Singh

We are sending an estimate and trust this meets the
requirement.

The car is in the Derby Al Garage and can be driven.

Sincerely
```

Check
Finished in time? Accurate? Including spacing to separate the parts of the letter? Try Workout 44.

LETTER LAYOUT

- Over seven days, Monday to Sunday, we had an excellent response, as follows:

Heading: ENQUIRIES

Day	Number	Contacts	Details received
1	10	2	
2	7	0	0
3	6	3	1
4	4	0	0
5	27	8	6
6	18	2	1
7	44	7	4

In addition, on the following Tuesday, there was a lively interest in such a project among the members of the Greenfingers Club, of whom 29 people offered help with contacts, acquaintances or research.

- We therefore agreed to proceed and to ask Mrs Carey to produce material on two houses of her choice, and that fees should be the same as paid for the first two manuscripts for the Local Gardens History series.

- We would pass to Mrs Carey the notes received from enquirers in the shop and ask her to fix a date when she would attend a meeting of the Greenfingers Club to collect contact details from members.

WPJ
(today's date)

Type this letter using A4 paper and an envelope (see Working Session 13):

Workout 44

TYPE

```
26 Fendry Avenue
Kirby
WREXHAM
CH31   1BT


3 March


Miss J H Vanghi
71 Drench Avenue
CRANDEIGH HEATH
HR31   1EX


Dear Judy

We have received a card advising that the curtains are
ready.  We can get them here next week and then Mr Jawed
can fetch them.  We are here every Tuesday, Wednesday,
Thursday and Friday.

Best wishes
```

Check

It's very important not to leave any mistakes in work which is going to be signed by somebody else – they would get the blame for your faults.

Did your remember to type the envelope?
Letter and envelope accurate?
Good. Move to **File.**

Made mistakes?
Take trouble to get it right before you move on.

File

File your paper copy for later use. Word processor users – index and save on disk.

Assignment 2

This in-tray assignment is work for Wayne Johnstone, Shops Manager at Greenery Ltd. Wayne looks after the books, cards and stationery areas in the garden centre shop.

The work here is:

- 2 pages of notes of a meeting
- family tree (you may adapt layout if you can't use the paper horizontally)
- letter to Mrs Carey, the author of a series of booklets on local gardens and their histories. (The booklets were written by arrangement with Greenery Ltd, and are a good selling line in the Greenery Garden Centre shop.)
- memo enclosing copies of all of the above to Lisa Menzies and Mrs Bentigon, who is General Manager of Greenery Ltd.

NOTES of meeting held (You supply the date)

See memo page 186

Present: Mrs G Bentigon
Lisa Menzies
Wayne P Johnstone

PROPOSAL FOR (all caps)
New series of booklets
booklets on

- The series of local gardens and their histories has been very popular and over six months the have had to be re-printed twice. The print run is being increased for a new order to be placed next month.

- Mrs Carey had asked if we would be interested in another series, this time on the gardeners who have worked at the local houses and maintained them, sometimes over several generations.

- To Before bringing this to your attention I had prepared a note on the likelihood of such a series and posted copies of it on cash desks and above the book shelves in the shop. The note asked customers to register any interest with the cashiers. We did it this way so that the cashiers, Sally and David, who could cd pass people on to ask if their customer had any knowledge of local people who had worked at the large country houses.

Retrieve

Find Letter 1 from your file (see Working Session 17).

Using a word processor?
Bring Letter 1 back to screen and make changes (see below); print with changes as Letter 2.

Using a typewriter?
Make changes to your paper copy and re-type as Letter 2.

Changes to make

- Type today's date.
- Address letter to:

Letter 2

Mr W M Smith
110 High Street
DENBIGH VALLEY
DE8 24C

- Type Dear Mr Smith.
- Change 'curtains' to 'coverings'.
- Change second sentence to:

We can deliver them, if required, on Monday, Tuesday or Wednesday of next week.

- Delete third sentence.
- Add new paragraph:

We shall be glad to hear which day you would like us to deliver them.

- Change 'Best wishes' to 'Yours sincerely'.
- Address an envelope to Mr Smith.

Check

Ask someone to read your letter and envelope.

If your checker finds fault, re-type so that your letter could be signed. File Letters 1 and 2.

Using a word processor?
You will not have to bring Letters 1 and 2 to screen again.
You can delete them from disk/memory if you wish.
Check the method with your tutor.

EDITING

THE KEYBOARD

THE firm GREENERY LTD has recently introduced a new range of products aimed at the gardener with only a small area at his/her disposal.

All of the tools are reasonably-priced but the quality of some is not what we have come to expect of this forceful company which started to trade only a few years ago and now has a firm foothold in the garden centre business as well as in its original base, as a manufacturer and factor of environmentally-friendly gardening products.

We now hear that GREENERY LTD is expanding into mainland Europe. Following an original and exciting exhibit in Paris, the firm is now planning to attend exhibitions at Bruparc Brussells and in the Grandeplec in Luxembourg.

We wish them well, but remind them that quality must be reliable, and new ranges must not be produced in a hurry, even when they are aimed at the customer at the lower end of their market. After all, "small is beautiful" and "look after the pennies and the pounds will look after themselves."

Please photocopy the above & send it to Lisa with the news I've asked you to write.

```
      8   9   0
        I   O   P
SHIFT LOCK          K   L   ;    RETURN
  SHIFT                      ,   .    SHIFT
              SPACE BAR
```

To reach up to **p** and **zero**: don't bend your wrist – just curl your fingertips slightly and move your hand forward a little.

Workout 45

TYPE
```
pop pops popped popple people poop pooped pores
poor poorly pour pours poured pouring
```

> Don't clench your fist.

```
please plus pleat pleasure prayer price press
priority permitted pence pests pounds pointed possible
hope application apologies apologise
```

```
10, 100, 20, 200, 30, 300, 40, 400, 50, 500
10 April 1990, 20 September 1990, 30 April 1990
Penelope Poppleton lives at 100 Poppy Place
```

Check

Remember to check figures particularly carefully.

The semi-colon

Check your own keyboard. The diagram at top of this page shows the semi-colon as a home key. If it's not there on your machine, use the chart on page 3 to see which finger you should use.

Workout 46

> One space after semi-colon.

TYPE
```
The party will comprise Paul, Penelope, Priscilla and
Poppy; in addition, Peter Pappingham will come later;
others may follow in due course.
```

Workout 47

TYPE
```
patina pretty pandas party political plenty
pristine parties policies payments priority
premium appointment disappointment deputise
epigram principium nepotism impropriety pop
```

Check

Have you copied these difficult words accurately? Yes? Excellent.

Having trouble? Unfamiliar words provide good copying practice. Have another try; concentrate on one letter at a time in the more difficult words.

WORKING SESSION 19

Secretary — tasks for you to do

Please send copies of the outline layout showing which products we can display ~~and~~ on the tables and so on to Jim Hallis and to Lisa Menzies.

Ask Jim if he sees any problems. And tell him I've told Stuart to contact him — see letter to Stuart.

The copy to Lisa is just for information.

Please add a note to Lisa, though to ~~tell~~ ask her if she's seen ~~about~~ the ~~attached~~ article from which the attached is an extract. Tell her also I've got a contact with ~~the~~ a member of the panel on Gardener's World. If she wants to make contact I can put her in touch. It might be useful to ~~ask~~ invite the panel to run their programme from our premises at ~~some~~ time in the future. I couldn't guarantee they'd accept but at least I could direct any invitation to the right quarters.

Also ask her if her department will be resp. for making the accom. arrangements for the people from my Department who are going to Bruparc. If not, who will be?

Thanks

KP

Retrieve

Find the form you filed in your Dictionary file (see Workout 38).

Using a word processor?

Bring the form back to screen. Add three more words, (Workout 48), save and print.

Using a typewriter?

Put the form back into your typewriter. Line up with the margin. Add three more words, see Workout 48.

Workout 48

Add to the form:

patina   ....

premium   ....

pristine   ....

Dictionary

Look up and write the meanings of all the words on your form.

Spacing

For handwritten entries, always leave at least one clear line space between dotted lines.

File

File your paper copy for later use.

Word processor users

You will not need to bring the form back to screen again. You can delete it from file/disk.

LAYOUT PROPOSAL - BRUPARC● BRUXELLES

Keep these spellings please

We shall need several copies - see memos

~~Exposition~~

──────── Entrance 1 (South) ────────

Photo-graphs and specifi-cations for Ride-on Mowers Abbey 602 and Parker 1100T

D I S P L A Y

Table 1 (D1100 Chukka)

Table 2 (RS 171 Dove)

Table 3 (B1x21 Bushbury)

D I S P L A Y

Photographs and Specifi-cations for 100 Paula and 285 & Bambi

Table 4 SHB386 Hanby

Table 5 (* Jukky)

Table 6 (MX162 *)

P A N E L S

P A N E L S

←──────── ENTRANCE 2 (NORTH) ────────

Room 1

Chair   Chair

D E S K   with phone

Chair

Room 2

Coffee Machine

Chairs (4)

BOARD ROOM TABLE

Chairs (4)

* *I've forgotten the number for Jukky + the name for MX162. They're on file (see Assignment 1 Section2)*
KP

Copy the memo below.
See page 92 for Style Guide to Memos.
Follow the layout here, including the spacing.

Memo 1

TYPE M E M O R A N D U M

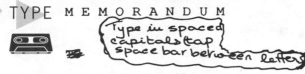

FROM   E Phillips

To   J Banks

ACCOUNTS REPORTS

                not
I shall/be able to let you have the reports you
require by the end of next week, after all.

                is being
The delay has been caused by a lack of information
from some of our branches. This was particularly true
of branches throughout Yorkshire, and it would appear
that there has been some difficulty with the Post
Office. I have contacted our local Post Office
Customer Service Manager; she is handling the matter
and keeping in touch.

In the meantime, the necessary details are being faxed
from our offices.
   to

You may receive complaints from some customers whose
payment receipts were also delayed during the last
fortnight. Please forward these to me, here.

Check
Ask someone to check your memo for you to see if they agree
with your version of the alterations, and that you have not left any
uncorrected error(s).

Made mistakes?
Re-type the memo, and when it's right, file it in your paper copy file.

Accurate first time?
Well done. File as Memo 1 in your file of paper copies.

Using a word processor?
After printing your hard copy, save Memo 1 so that you can bring
it back to screen when required.

House style
Some organisations like 'from' and 'to' in the order above. Others
prefer 'to' to come first. Check and follow style.

INTRODUCING MEMOS

Memo to

Tim

Kevin

BRUPARC/~~K~~ BRUXELLES

I attach a copy of the outline layout with the details
~~we agreed~~ for the display panels and tables. I've
sent it off to Stuart and he'll no doubt be in
touch.

If Stuart wants to use any of the material we kept
from the Green World exhibition is it really
~~suitably~~ preserved? It may not be possible, of course,
but I would like to re-use as much of it as we
can. Perhaps you'll make ~~sure~~ over the next
few days.   (it's OK)

When we do start on the photography for Bruparc
it will be better this time to highlight the edges
of blades, etc as I think we all agreed last
time. Can we make sure what Stuart thinks
about colour? ~~before we start~~ We can have this
process done in the Workshop. Harry Brent
is very good at that sort of work. You may
remember what he did for the catalogue
photographs last autumn.

In view of the amount of normal production work now coming
on to the Department, I want to schedule this
promotion work.   Let me know if you think these
times are appropriate:

Bruparc		
Photographs	3 × ½ day	
Models	5 × 1 day	
Packing	3 × ½ day	
Checking	2 × 1 day	

'Kleenwater'	
Packing	2 × ½ day

Look at your keyboard to find the dash key. Then look at the chart on page 3 to see which finger you should use.

Using the dash to punctuate sentences
Workout 49

> The dash is separate from the words.

TYPE

(Leave one space either side)

```
There will never - well, hardly ever - be another
chance.
We shall be there - most of us - by the time required.
How do we know if the office will - or ought to - be
open throughout the month?
```

Instead of the word 'to'
Workout 50

TYPE

{No space here}

The show is open 11 am – 4 pm each day 3 – 7 July. We expect to be there with you 12 noon – 2.30 pm on 6 March.

The journey Portsmouth – London will take us 3 – 4 hours.

The Poppleton Restaurant will be closed 12 – 14 December.

{Leave one space either side of the dash}

When the dash is used for 'to', some people prefer to have no spaces: 'The show is open 11 am–4 pm each day'.

Workout 51

TYPE

We shall be glad if you will let us know – by Thursday of next week if possible – which days you will be attending the exhibition. The show is open 11 am – 4 pm Monday – Friday and 12 noon – 8 pm Saturday.

If you are able to do so we would like you to be there Monday – Wednesday. Our own staff – Jane and Anne – will be able to cope with the other times.

Check
Read through Workouts 49–51 again. Can you spot when the dash is used for the two different purposes:

- to punctuate sentences
- for the word 'to'?

WORKING SESSION 20

Assignment 1

This is an in-tray exercise in which you are producing work for Kevin Percy, Production Manager at Greenery Ltd. The work in Assignment 1, Section Two, was also for Kevin, so you will have some details on file.

The work here is:

- a letter to Stuart Diamond; you already have a file on the 'Kleenwater' project
- a memo to a Tim Desmet
- revisions to the diagram produced by Stuart and Tim
- memos to accompany the revised diagram to Jim Hallis and Lisa
- an extract from an article in a gardening magazine with comments by Kevin.

Letter to Stuart Diamond (You have the address on file)

Dear S—

BRUPARCK BRUXELLES

I now return to you the outline layout with additions showing which products we can display on the tables and the material we would like on the display panels.

We have some of the work still available from the Greenworld exhibition. We have stored it in 'exhibition rig' so that it sld still be ok for use. Jim will contact you to arrange an inspection.

We shall be crating the models for 'Kleenwater' next week. Do you want to add anything to the original packing instructions? If so, please contact Jim before Tuesday pm.

The Brussells project is quite exciting. We are all looking forward to it as this is the first time Production personnel have attended such an event. The Paris one seems to have gone well, and we have today received in Production Department the first order from Marchelle et Cie, Aix-en-Provence. Lisa tells me there are more on the way from two other companies in France and at least one in Switzerland. Let's hope Belgian firms are equally interested in us and our products!

No doubt you will be along also to take new photographs of the mowers and chainsaws. I shall be glad if you can give us a week's notice if you need things set up here.

Yours sinc— KPetc

179

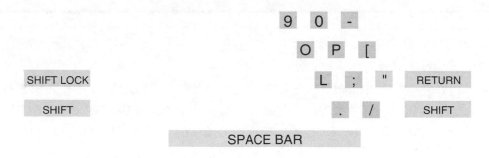

Look at your own keyboard to find the double quotes key. Then look at the chart on page 3 to see which finger you should use. This key usually works with the shift key.

Conversation

Quotation marks must be used twice: once at the start and again at the end of the quoted word(s).

Workout 52

> No space between word and mark.

Watch where the full stops are typed.

TYPE

```
"You are invited to tea" said Mary.
"Thanks" replied Jason.
Mary replied "Well, perhaps Tuesday would be a good
idea".
"I shall need to know for sure."
"Well, I can let you know when I see you on Saturday."
"Thanks."
```

Full stops and quotes

If part of the sentence is not quoted, then the full stop goes after the last quote marks (see first three sentences in Workout 52).

When all of the sentence is part of the quotation, the full stop goes before the last quotation marks.

Check

As well as word accuracy, did you type all the punctuation exactly as shown?

Yes?
Good, now move to Memo 2.

No?
Have another try; concentrate on the punctuation. When you're sure you can get it right, move on.

Step by step

NVQs at all levels are made up of units. Each unit covers one part of the work (eg 'Filing', 'Mail Handling'). You can have a certificate for one or more units even if you aren't ready, or don't want to go for, the full qualification.

In the NVQ Business Administration Level 2 (Secretarial), Unit 16 is 'Text Processing'.

When you pass RSA exams (Parts 1 and 2) at Stage II or Stage III in Typewriting Skills or in Word Processing, you have already shown competence which will count towards this unit.

Other exams give you the chance to show you are competent in part of a unit (called an Element). For example, RSA Stage I Typewriting Skills and/or Word Processing, count towards Element 3.1 in Business Administration Levels 1 and 2.

Further details

NVQs are run by RSA and other awarding bodies, and you can enter for them in the same way as for exams, that is, through a centre which may be a college, school or your workplace.

Your tutor/supervisor will be able to give you full details of the syllabus for the qualification in which you are interested.

If you are working alone and would like more information about RSA schemes, the address to write to is:

RSA Examinations Board, Westwood Way, COVENTRY CV4 8HS

The work in Section Three

In this section there are five assignments.

The aim of the section is to prepare you for the sort of text processing work done in offices.

Type this memo, which you will need to keep on file. Make all the corrections shown.

M E M O R A N D U M

Memo 2

TO   Bernice Happness

FROM   Harry Wells

(Today's date)

CATALOGUE COPY

Here are the copy sentences for the ~~four~~ *five* pages we talked about at our last meeting.

Below item A on page 17 - "This pretty Victorian style blouse is available in azure blue, raspberry and apricot".

To the ~~i~~side of item C on page ~~24~~ *28* - "One of our most popular items, this jacket is now reduced in price. Full details on page ~~27~~".

Above item~~s~~ G on page 36 *30* - "Available in sizes 8 - 16".

For page 390 we have decided to add to the last sentence - "and is now available in all sizes and colours".

On page 44 we want to delete the last few words - "and will suit all tastes".

Check
Ask someone to read your memo. Have you made the corrections properly? Have you copied the punctuation accurately? Would your checker sign it if he or she were Harry?

Accurate?
Excellent! File your Memo 2 in your paper copy file.

Need to re-type?
It's always worth taking the trouble to get your work accurate. When it's OK, file Memo 2 in your file of paper copies.

Using a word processor?
Save Memo 2 so that you can recall it to screen.

House style
In this memo 'to' comes first. Check and follow house style.

MEMO LAYOUT

THE KEYBOARD

The qualifications aimed at office workers, including secretaries, are now:

▶ Business Administration Level 1

▶ Business Administration Level 2 (plus options to show competence in specialist work such as general secretarial or financial, medical, legal and agricultural secretarial and administration)

▶ Administration Level 3.

The differences

Conventional exams are designed to allow you to show your knowledge and skill in one or more particular 'subjects' which are an important part of the type of work you want to do.

NVQs show that you have proved you can put your exam success to good use at work and have gained competence in other parts of the work. For example, in offices you may be asked to:

▶ use a typewriter and a word processor

▶ make photocopies

▶ use the telephone and a switchboard

▶ keep records

▶ open the mail, send out mail including using a franking machine

▶ send fax messages

▶ and to do a variety of other jobs normally thought of as part of office work.

Look at your own keyboard to find the colon key. Then look at the chart on page 3 to see which finger you should use. You may need to use the shift key with the colon.

'As follows'
The colon is often used to mean 'as follows'.

Workout 53

TYPE

```
There are two of them: Joan and Sylvester.

We have these environmentally-friendly goods
available:

washing powder
toilet soap
tissues

The disco will be held on three days: Monday,
Tuesday and Thursday.

Lipsticks are supplied in three sizes priced:
£1.98, £3.45, £4.75.

Brooches as modelled are sold at: Norton
Gallery, Jimjam Shops, Brighouse Boutique.
```

Leave a clear line before a list

One space after a colon when in a sentence.

Check
Did you separate the short paragraphs by one clear linespace, as shown? Have you double-checked the prices?

Accurate?
Very good. Now move on to Letter 3.

Made mistakes?
Have another try at the paragraphs in which you made mistakes. When you're confident you can get it right, move on to Letter 3.

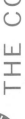

Qualifications

There are now two sorts of qualification:

▶ conventional, single-subject examinations

▶ National Vocational Qualifications (NVQs).

Conventional exams

In text processing skills, for example, RSA runs exams in:

▶ Core Text Processing Skills – for the learner (this exam can be taken using a typewriter or a word processor)

▶ Typewriting Skills, Word Processing, Audio Transcription and Shorthand Transcription:

Stage I – for the beginner in this type of employment

Stage II – for the secretarial employee who can cope with general office work on his/her own

Stage III – for the senior secretary, who would expect to be given any new or particularly complicated jobs.

NVQs

These have more recently been introduced by the National Council for Vocational Qualifications. At present they are run at five levels:

Level 1 – for those with basic knowledge of an occupation, such as business, and with skills to cope with routine or predictable jobs

Level 2 – for people with job experience, able to work more on their own and to take on longer and more difficult tasks

Level 3 – for more senior employees with a wide range of skills, able to deal with complex and unusual tasks, including supervising others

Level 4/5 – those working at management level.

Type the letter and envelope. File your paper copy of Letter 3 in your file.

Using a word processor?
You will not need to retrieve Letter 3 on the screen so you may delete it from file/disk.

Letter 3

```
"Hazleholme"
22 Brensham Avenue
Cransham Common
Southport   PR9 33TS
```

(Type today's date here)

```
Ferrybridge Health Hydro
Yoxton Delvton
CHRISTCHURCH
Dorset    BH23 6TY
```

```
FOR ATTENTION OF: MISS D J OLDERWAY
```

```
Dear Sirs
```

```
I left my sports bag in Room 221 when I left Ferrybridge
on Friday of last week.  When I telephoned today, Jayne
Olderway told me the bag is being held in your Lost
Property Office.
```

```
I have asked my friend, Amanda Clekson, to collect my bag
for me when she comes to Ferrybridge next month.  The
details Jayne asked me to confirm are:
```

```
Name and address of my friend: Amanda Clekson
                               12 Keysham Close
                               Cransham Major
                               Southport   PR9 1TT
```
(start each line at same point)

```
Dates booked at Ferrybridge:   Monday to Friday 12-16 of
                               next month.
```

Description of my bag: blue with white logo.

```
Yours faithfully
```

```
James Brenton
```

WORKING SESSION 22

5.30 pm   Check into Rochester Hotel
7.30 pm   Dinner with Alan Goodly (Mannerings'
           Managing Director). (Rosie Moreland
           and Derek Buford to attend.)

Friday, 6 Dec

10.30 am   Arrive Manchester Piccadilly to
           catch 10.54 to Chichester.

**Now you're ready to move to Section Three, which gives
you the chance to assess the competence you've gained
since starting this book.**

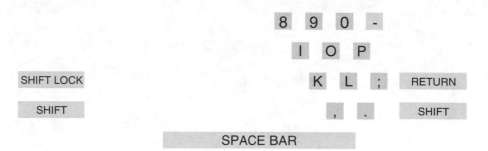

In Working Session 20 you found the dash key.

Use the same key for the hyphen.

The hyphen joins two words, or two parts of a word, together. There must not be any space round it; that would have the opposite effect by splitting the word(s) apart.

Workout 54

TYPE
```
in-house pre-eminent off-shore out-station on-stream
mid-day co-operative re-engagement pre-ordained
Mrs Ponsonby-Splinge will attend the half-day show.
The records contained details of on-job experience as
well as off-job courses at College.
This person has worked as a part-time shop assistant
after 4 years as a full-time shop manager.
```

Not the same
In the next workout you are typing hyphens; you are also using the same key to type dashes. They are not the same thing.

Workout 55

Spaces round dashes but not hyphens.

TYPE
```
We all intend - to a greater or lesser degree - to co-
operate with the Off-Shore Manager. He will be
arriving tomorrow and will be conducting in-house
interviews for 2 - 3 days.
```

Check
As well as general word accuracy in Workouts 54 and 55, make sure you haven't left any spaces within words.

Made mistakes?
It's worth trying again and getting it right before moving on.

Accurate?
Executives value your skills if you can be relied upon for accurate use of punctuation.

THE HYPHEN

5.00 pm Paddington Stn to catch 5.20 to
         Oxford.

7pm   Check in to Portland Hotel (Leamington
         Place)

Tues, 4 Dec

10am   Redwells Bk Shp for signing
         session. (Derek Burford to attend)

1.30   Vixen Radio Studio for interview with
         Cleo Capitello (on air 2-15 - 3pm)

5.00pm   Arrive Oxford Railway Stn to catch 5.17
         to B'ham.

7.30pm   Check into Shelton Hotel.

Wed, 5 Dec

10.30am Riverstones / B'ham for signing session (Maria
         Beefley to attend).

12.00pm W. Midlands / BBC Radio Stn for interview
         with Winston Cooperard. On air
         12.45 - 1.45.

7-30pm   Solihull ~~Com~~ community Centre to speak to Rotary Club

Thursday, 5 Dec

9.00am   Check out of Shelton Hotel

10.00 am Birmingham Railway Stn to catch
         10.21 to Manchester.

2.30pm   Mannerings Bk Shop / Manchester for signing
         session (Rosie Moreland to attend)

Type this memo. It has dashes and hyphens. Make sure you know the difference.

Memo 3

MEMORANDUM

TO   P Appleton

FROM   J Wentworth   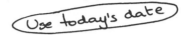 *Use today's date*

SALES CONFERENCE WEEK

I attach the summary of activities to be undertaken.

Please let me have your requirements under the
following headings:

Accom(M)odation
Food - staff, on-stand entertainment and off-stand
entertainment
Drinks - on-stand only
Travel allowances - mileage and fares
Expenses 14 - 18 January and 19 - 26 January.

You will remember it was agreed at the last meeting
that cash would be issued only for amounts up to £50;
invoices to be accepted for amounts £51- £150; and any
sum over this to be specially sanctioned.

This reminds everyone to look out for an enclosure.

Enc ← *Leave a line clear then type Enc at left margin*

Check

Ask someone to read your memo and check:

- are all words accurate including hyphens?
- is the punctuation copied accurately including dashes?

Accurate?
If your checker would be prepared to sign it, file your paper copy.

Made mistakes?
Don't begrudge the time to get punctuation and other refinements accurate. It'll pay off in the long run.

When you're confident you can get it right, file your paper copy.

Using a word processor?
You won't need to bring Memo 3 back to screen.

WORKING SESSION 23

Simone Marvell's promotional tour for
Hollywood Lives

(change to 24 hr clock)

Itinerary

Sat, 1 Dec

Sec:
Spell out abbreviation
stn = station
Bk Shp = Book Shop
B'ham = Birmingham

Bk Shp

10.30 am   Riverstones, Chichester for
(signing session)

2.30 pm   lunch with bk. shp. mgr.

4 pm   BBC Sussex Radio (U.C) studio – interview
with Roger Waverley (on air 5.15 →
5.45)

Sun, 2 Dec

6 pm   limo to pick up Simone Marvell from house and
take to Chichester Railway Stn

6.35   Train to London, Victoria

8.30   Check into Milton Hotel

9.00   Dine in hotel restaurant (Rosie Matford,
Sheila Houston, Derek Burford, (BURFORD) to attend)
Perminder
Rahima   (PERMINDER RAHIMA)

Mon, 3 Dec

(= C10)

10.00am   Mannering Book Shop for signing session.
(Rosie Moreland to attend)

2.30pm   arrive Riverbank Conference Centre to give
presentation to reps.

173

ASSIGNMENT 4

Look at your own keyboard. Find the apostrophe key. Then use the chart on page 3 to see which finger you should use.

Apostrophe and s

In Workout 56 an apostrophe and an **s** have been added to the words 'dog' 'owner' and 'doctor' to show ownership, e.g. the collar of the dog; the owner of the dog; the car of the doctor.

Workout 56

TYPE
```
The dog's collar shows the owner's name and address.
The dog's owner is a doctor.
The doctor's car is in the drive at the surgery.
```

In Workout 57 an apostrophe has been added but no **s** is needed because 'cats' 'girls' and 'nurses' are plurals and already have an **s**.

Workout 57

TYPE
```
The cats' food was in the blue bowls.
The girls' uniforms were all at the cleaners.
The nurses' roster was posted on the wall at the Nurses'
Hostel.
```

In Workout 58 an apostrophe and an **s** are added to the words 'men' 'sheep' and 'children'. Even though these words are plurals, they do not already have an **s**.

Workout 58

TYPE
```
The men's washroom is at the end of the hall.
Jim was called a wolf in sheep's clothing.
The children's socks are all in the wash.
```

Type Workout 59 putting in apostrophes (there are six missing):

Workout 59

TYPE
```
The executives file was ready for him.
Mandys stationery was put ready on the desk.
The ten boys caps were left at Joans house.
"Charnley Six" is a womens club; the members caps and
blazers are designed by Clancy.
```

THE APOSTROPHE

THE KEYBOARD

Gary Stevenson
'Turnpike'
2 The ~~Crospes~~ Crofts
Winnersh
Wokingham
RG12 6HW

> Please prepare
> an envelope for this
> letter

Dear Gary

Thanks for agreeing to undertake the progreading of
Hollywood Lives.

I ~~am sending~~ ~~enclose~~ the proofs herewith, together w. the original
manuscript, ~~undersea~~ ~~over~~. Please return all to me by 27 July.
TO ~~following~~ last Wed's conversation, let me
recap on the programme of work we have for you
over the coming months:

Book title	Date	Type of work
Marilyn - the Legend	9 Aug.	progreading
Fitness Can be Fun	2 Sept.	copy-editing
Fitness Can be Fun	10 Nov.	progreading
Traditional Knitwear	16 Aug.	progreading
Make-up for Brides	30 Sept.	copy-editing

(NB These dates are approx.)

On the question of payment, I bel. we agreed on
a revised rate of £10.50 per hour for future work.

I was sorry to hear you felt payment for yr. last
job was unduly delayed. I'm not resp. for settling
freelancers' invoices, but I know that it's co.
policy not to pay before 30 days from ~~receipt~~ receipt
of invoice.

Anyway, enjoy reading H ⟶ L — . It's a
fascinating book!

Yours sncly

Marion Beezley
Senior
Assistant Editor

SECTION TWO

Apostrophe for missing letters

In Workout 60 the apostrophes show that words are shortened.
The apostrophe is at the point where letters are missing.

Workout 60

TYPE
```
I didn't let Ms Malley know that we can't go.
The new video isn't ready yet.  I don't know when it will
be available for sale.
It's too late to go to the party.  I'm going home.
```

Workout 61

Type and include apostrophes where letters are missing (there are
6 apostrophes needed):

TYPE
```
JOANNE:  "We dont always believe what were told."
PHIL:    "Who said that?"
RANJIT:  "Ive no idea."
JOANNE:  "I did.  Who did you think was speaking?"
PHIL:    "I couldnt see you, but I did know Ranjit
          hadnt spoken."
RANJIT:  "Well, theres no need to argue about it."
```

Answers to Workout 59
The executive's file was ready for him.
Mandy's stationery was put ready on the desk.
The ten boys' caps were left at Joan's house.
"Charnley Six" is a women's club; the members' caps and
blazers are designed by Clancy.

Answers to Workout 61
JOANNE: "We don't always believe what we're told."
PHIL: "Who said that?"
RANJIT: "I've no idea."
JOANNE: "I did. Who did you think was speaking?"
PHIL: "I couldn't see you, but I did know Ranjit hadn't spoken."
RANJIT: "Well, there's no need to argue about it."

THE APOSTROPHE

Assignment 4

In this assignment you are again working for Mondori Publishing. Your principal, Maria Beefley, is writing to an editorial freelancer, and sending an internal memo to the picture researcher. You also have to type up a complicated itinerary for a promotional author tour.

MEMO

typist: change picture to photo th'out

To: Ahmed Khalif (Picture researcher)
From: Maria Beefley

leave as 'Picture'

Hollywood Lives : Picture fees

Unfortunately it looks as though we will have to cut the number of pictures in this book. However, the ~~The~~ picture fees we have been quoted are far too ~~expen~~ expensive /and our budget simply won't accom. them.

Unless you can renegotiate with the picture libraries, we will def. have to lose the following:

inset 5 spares
no. 22   Demi Moore holding baby
no. 28   Michael Douglas with Jessica Lange
no. 12   Antony Hopkins on Silence of the Lambs set
no. 18   Elizabeth Taylor in Beverley Hills Mansion

I wl. let you know of any further cuts when I've agreed ~~them~~ with the author.
original
As you know our ∧ intention was to include 80 full- colour and 120 black/ and white We felt that this was the minimum number of pictures required ~~required~~ given our target market and what our competitors have produced.

SECTION TWO

Look at your own keyboard. Find the exclamation mark. It usually needs the shift key.

You don't need to type the exclamation mark very often, but it's important to be able to find it easily when necessary.

Workout 62

Type the following. Leave the same number of spaces after the exclamation mark as you do after a full stop.

TYPE
```
Do not open this door! It is not appropriate!
We could not hear ourselves speak above the applause!
Protect the environment and take your litter home!
TRY OUR BARGAINS! THE UNREPEATABLE SALES EVENT!
```

Note: Some people choose to leave a space *before* typing the exclamation mark. Whatever you decide, always use the same style.

Workout 63

Type the following draft for an article in a magazine:

TYPE

Type/print in double linespacing

NATIONAL PARK SAFARIS

Several parks run motoring safaris to see wild animals in their natural habitat. Each park has its own vehicles and it's compulsory ~~that~~ for visitors to travel in them and not in their own cars. ~~or on foot.~~ You must never walk!

There are wardens at each enclosure and each driver must follow the wardens' directions. This means not all of the visitors' routes are exactly the same. The route may be altered at a moment's notice if, say, the wardens spot animals at a waterhole but do not want too many buses to approach, for fear of scaring the animals away.

EXCLAMATION MARK

WORKING SESSION 25

SUMMER COLLECTION: MODELS

→ caps + bold
or u/lined, pls

NAME	HEIGHT	EYES	HAIR	COMMENTS
1. Penny Ising	5'9	Br	DK Br	
2. * Kathy Miles	6'0	Bl	Blo	Sec: pls write out in full Blo = Blond DK Br = Dark Brown Bla = Black Br = Brown Bl = Blue
3. Sophie Bhola	5'8	Br	Bla	
4. Efuru Nwapa	5'9	Br	DK Br	
5. Nikki Franks	5'9	Bl	Blo	
6. Imogen White	5'8	Bl	Red	
7. Kate O'Reilly	5'9	Green	DK Br	
8. Bess Robertson	6'0	Br	Bla	
9. Nnu Ego (NNU)	5'9	Br	DK Br	
10. Jagua Nana (JAGUA)	5'8	Br	DK Br	
11. Ali Glover	5'9	Green	Bla	
12. Sarah Timms.	6'1	Br	DK Br	
13. Karen Cartwright	5'8	Bl	Straw Blo	
14. Melanie Peroni	5'9	Green	DK Br	
15. Claudya Mindel	5'8	Bl	Bl	
16. Odele Capen	5'9	Br	Blo	
17. Salma Hussain	6'0	Br	DK Br	
18. Sharon Hadman	5'8	Bl	DK Br	

Sec: pls type up as ruled table

names put in alpha order

* in-house model

Look at your own keyboard. Find the bracket keys. Then look at the chart on page 3 to see which fingers you should use. You will need to use the shift key with brackets.

Workout 64
No space between bracket and the word to which it applies.

TYPE
We (23 Crypt Club members) will arrive in time (at 6 pm).

There are many (upwards of 100) who want tickets. The prizewinners (Joan for Hairdressing and Clarence for Beauty Care) will be presented with their prizes by Mrs B T Bradley (Manager, Barnet Branch) at 7.30 pm.

The programme is in five sections:

1) Introduction Speeches
2) Demonstrations by Colleges
3) Presentations
4) Demonstrations by prizewinners
5) Buffet supper.

Check
Brackets are used quite often in business correspondence, particularly with numbering. You may find it better to look for these keys as you type them.

Timing
Try to type the following in no more than two minutes:

TYPE
Please note that all advertisements must be registered with the Administrative Officer before being placed on this Notice Board.

As well as advertisements, this rule includes requests for accommodation.

Check
Did you finish in two minutes? If so, you are working at about 15 words a minute, with increased accuracy.

Made mistakes?
You can't really claim to be typing at 15 words a minute unless you are also accurate.

When you're sure you can get it right, move on to Letter 4.

Vivek Khatkar
Production Manager
Excadia Fashion Group
Production Premises
Tipton Industrial Park
Hull
HU15 9ZG

(Use informal style – keep abbreviations)

Dr. Vivek

I wd. like to arrange an appt. for me to visit the prod. factory at some point in the next two weeks.

This visit/will ~~also~~ give me the opp. of looking into the stitching problems w. (style 201... (sec. check number from yr file) keyboard Section Assignment 4) the Dupion strapless silk ~~evening dress~~/ I'm meant to be visiting a retailer in York at 4pm on the Wednesday after next (sec: add date). Could I see you in the morning?

I think we ought to discuss some of the new designs which you wl. be mfring (MANUFACTURING) in the coming months. I anticipate that one or two of these garments, including the short chiffon shift dress, which was previewed at our last design meeting, will present new prod. (PRODUCTION) difficulties for your machinists, and I'd like to see if we can devise a new method of working to counter likely problems before they occur.// I'll be bringing various garments and fabrics with me to show the retailer, so if there's anything from our new collection you'd like a closer look at, let me know and I'll throw that in the car, too!

Do get in contact ~~as soon as possible~~ asap, so that I can confirm my meeting in York.

Yours sely

Vivien Peters
Designer

Type this letter and prepare an envelope:

16 New Street
Ferrybridge
BIRMINGHAM
B96 2SX

Leave 2 inches at the top for printed letter head

(Today's date)

Dear Mike

Thanks for your help with the photo sessions. I know now that you've given Jo and Bill advice and help over and above what was originally asked of you.

Keep the informal style throughout

I understand you have intimated you don't intend to increase your fee, and my directors have asked me to say how much they appreciate this.

I'm sure your goodwill will reap its reward (even if it's not this year)!

Wishing you every success,
Yours sincerely

Check
Ask someone to check your letter and envelope for you.

Have you used apostrophes and brackets as shown? Is your typing accurate? Are new paragraphs and different parts of the letter clearly shown with space between them?

Accurate first time?
Excellent. File your paper copy in your file.

Made mistakes?
Take the time to get it right before filing your work.

Using a word processor?
You won't need to bring Letter 4 back to screen.

House style
Some organisations use informal style. Others expect you to type such abbreviations in full. Check and follow house style.

Assignment 3
Once again you're working for Escadia Fashion Ltd. There is a
letter from Vivien Peters (the designer) to the production factory
and a memo and form from her arranging a model selection.

M E M O ← (spaced caps)

TO : Robert Meecham, Rose Alphouse et Karen Dallas,
Stephen North

FROM: Vivien Peters

RE: Summer Collection : Models

Next Wednesday 18 shortlisted models from the Chic
Agency will be coming to the studio so that we
can make our final selection to use at our
Summer collection shows (shows).

~~We will follow our usual selection procedure~~

The girls will arrive at 10.30am when we will
~~have~~ hold an informal meeting with them (coffee
and biscuits to be available)

Each girl will then be given one garment from the
collection to model for us.

Pls may I ~~re iterate~~ emphasise that it is imperative that the
models we select have the right 'look' for this
particular collection.

All the clothes from evening wear right through to (therefore)
swimwear have a very strong ethnic flavour, + i.e. the
model must be able to carry off this exotic look with
flair.

To make the selection process a little easier, pls find
attached a ~~pro~~ list detailing each model, for yr.
info. + comments. (NB sec. pls type up list + circulate
with memo).

After ~~viewing~~ you have seen all 18 girls, pls list your chosen
8 models in order of preference on the attached
list.

Thanks.

Don't rest on your laurels

Whenever you strike problems with keying, use the Error Clinic on pages 201–7. There can be fun in drilling as well as the reward of getting it right.

To end the Keyboard Section, here are five work assignments to try before launching into Section One.

These assignments become more difficult with more work to be completed within the target time.

This work is typical of some of the tasks in RSA Core Text Processing Exams. Candidates for NVQ Level 1 Business Administration might also be expected to type this sort of work.

Assignment 1

This is an in-tray exercise. You are producing work for Michael Schreiber, a freelance exhibitions organiser.

The work here is:

- a letter to Lisa Menzies, the exhibitions manager of an environmental products firm which is planning an exhibition stand at a trade fair
- a note to a possible buyer arranging a meeting.

You should aim to type two accurate letters with copies and envelopes within 45 minutes.

THE KEYBOARD

Memo from Philip Coates
    to Jim Clark   Ref PC/AGM

ANNUAL GENERAL MEETING

I am enclosing a copy of the letter I
am sending to Mr G Roberts (address as
letter).
I sh be glad if you wl take care of
all the expense claims as they come in.
The accounts
All the for publicity material wl be
passed to you shortly. This takes the
~~publicity material is on its way~~
lion's share of the budget.

                      good
The choice of a hotel in London was
felt to be important because our
shareholders come from overseas,
as well as from all over the United Kingdom.

Please let me have a breakdown of
costs as soon as possible.

Mr Roberts has given a substantial
discount because of the increased
business.

letter to

Lisa Menzies
Greenery Ltd
7A Pilger Street
Taunton
Someset
SA17 8HH

108 Bilton Street
Dorking
Surrey
DO1 1EY

Dear Lisa

GREEN WORLD CONFERENCE, SAN FRANCISCO

Thank you for your recent letter, asking me to organise your company stand at this exhibition. I am happy to accept the terms you suggest.

I have already spoken to the organisers and provisionally agreed to book stand C7. This is within the price range you suggested and is in the main hall, ground floor. The organisers can't allow you to sell products from the stand, but have said the product demonstration won't infringe any regulations.

I have written to Bill Myto today suggesting a meeting.

Yours sincerely

Michael Schreiber

THE KEYBOARD

Our ref PC/AW

URGENT

Mr G Roberts
The Brittania Hotel
Broad Lane
LONDON   SW1 6AY

Take 2 extra copies including 1 to be routed to Jim Clark. Also, please address 2 labels —
1 for Gary
1 for Jim

Dr ~~Mr Roberts~~ Gary

ANNUAL GENERAL MEETING

Thank you for yr note wh I recd yesterday. ~~I was pleased to get your letter yesterday informing me about the final arrangements.~~ In view of yr concern about safety, we sh arrange for ~~two of~~ our own security staff to attend // to search bags as people enter the room. With regard to the final plans for the CHee's meeting on Tues*, we sh require overnight accom for 23 people. Any requests for extras must be refd to me.

On the evening before the AGM *(type in full)*, we sh need a sep room to be set aside for our own staff to set up exhibitions of company publications. A finger buffet has already been ordered for 5.30 pm to keep us going until dinner, wh has been ordered for 8 pm in the Magellan Room.

Please order taxis to take the staff home immed after they finish setting up the displays. All exps) will be settled by our Accounts Department and I am sending a copy of this letter to Jim Clark in confirmation of this arrangement. Staff have been warned they will need ~~receipts~~ to claim exps. from Jim.

Yours sinc'ly

Philip Coates
Company Secretary

* please add the date for Tues of next week

SECTION TWO

letter to

Bill Myto
Earthstores
88 Bleeker Hill
San Francisco 21008
California

108 Bilton Street
Dorking
Surrey
DOI IEY

Keep informal
style with
apostrophes where I
use them.   MS

Dear Bill

Amazingly, it's / already Green World time again, and
I may have an interesting contact for you.

I'm planning the exhibition stand for a
company called Greenery Ltd which plans
and landscapes environmentally—friendly areas
of any size for office complexes, housing
projects etc. Last year you were talking
about planning picnic gardens for each of
your stores. Is this still / likely ? If so, get in
touch before the exhibition and I'll arrange
for you to meet the Greenery Ltd people
when they come over to set up their
exhibition stand.

I hope to see you in any case. I owe
you a lunch!

Regards

Michael Schreiber

43

FINANCIAL

~~PRAXI FINANCE~~ INFORMATION SHEET

Annual General Meeting

This will be held at the Britannie Hotel, Broad Lane, London on
22 April at 11 am. The Notice of Meeting showing the business
to be dealt with and note's of explaination, will be circulated
with this report.

The meeting will be held on the ground floor, with the
enterance from Broad Lane. The hotel is served by tube and bus
sevices and parking is available underneath the hotel.

The doors will be open from 10 am onwards when tea, coffeee and
biscuits will be served. Help will be available for disabled
people.

Other improtant dates is given below:

This para in double linespacing

Timetable of Key Dates

1	22 April	Annual General Meeting
2	11 May	Payment of final dividend to shareholder's on the register at 20 March
3	3 May	~~Half-yearly~~ *Quarterly* results announced
4	4 August	Half-yearly results announced in national press
5	12 October	Payment of interim dividend

If you have special enqiries please write to us and address
your enquiry to the Registrar Services Section. Please give
your full name address and share certificate number.

If you should change your name, please send your share
certificate and other documents, eg marraige ~~lines~~. For lost
certificates please enclose a £10 search fee.

Praxi shares can be bought or sold by post. This service are
provided by Shareline, a member of the banking association.
Details of our other services is given in our leaflets. please
obtain these from your local branch.

Highlights of our report and accounts will be available on
audio tape for blind or partially sited clients. Contact us at
the Public Relations Departement.
Leave 6 clear linespaces

Our register are a public document and it is possible that
clients may have received mail from other organisations as a
result of this. Please contact us if you wish us to withhold
your name.

Assignment 2

This is an in-tray exercise. You are producing work for Sue Golding, a marketing manager for BlottCo, a design company.

The work here is:

- a memo to a designer
- a letter with envelope to Michael Schreiber, a freelance exhibition organiser who is setting up BlottCo's exhibition stand at a German trade fair called Design-Ex
- a draft company description for the exhibition catalogue.

You should aim to type an accurate letter, envelope, memo and article within one hour.

You will find appropriate letter heads for this assignment and all the others at the end of the book. Cut out the pages and carefully photocopy them.

 Max Scott

Sue Golding

DESIGN-EX, STUTTGART

Just to let you know that Michael Schreiber has agreed to organise the stand for us and act as interpreter. I've written to him today to confirm.

We should meet when you return from holiday to discuss display panels, and whether we take the desk-top publishing demonstration kit or not. Michael says he can explain it in German and Russian!

THE KEYBOARD

> Please rearrange into alphabetical order of surname within each section, eg:
>
> Jose Carreras 1 May 31 July 3000
> . . . . . etc.
>
> Rule as shown.

PRAXI MUSIC

Recordings by popular artists have been targeted for promotion over the coming months.

STYLE	PROMOTION PERIOD		AMOUNT* BUDGETED £
	FROM	TO	
Classical			
Luciano Pavarotti	1 March	31 May	3000
Placido Domingo	1 April	30 June	3000
Yehudi Menuhin	1 March	31 May	2500
Paul Tortelier	1 May	31 July	2000
James Galway	1 June	31 August	2000
Jose Carreras	1 May	31 July	3000
Nigel Kennedy	1 April	30 June	2500
Popular	The exact promotion period has still to be decided. It will depend partly on the production of pop videos. These will be broadcast at peak television viewing times. Full details will be available in the next few weeks.		
Kate Bush			4000
Tom Jones			2000
Cliff Richard			3000
Tina Turner			3500
Jazz			
Billie Holliday	1 March	31 May	1500
Ella Fitzgerald	1 April	30 June	2000
Louis Armstrong	1 May	31 July	1500

* The maximum figure is shown. This should not be exceeded without prior approval.

SECTION TWO

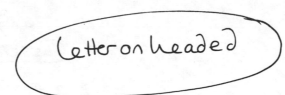
Letter on headed

Michael Schreiber
108 Bilton Street
Dorking
SURREY
DO1 7EY

envelope or
label needed

Dear Michael

Thanks for coming to see me yesterday.

I am writing to confirm that we would like you to
undertake the following on behalf of BlottCo Design
(all dates and times to be finalised next week) :

1. Drive the company van to Stuttgart and back,
   handle all export and customs paperwork and set up
   the stand at Design-ex.
2. ~~Offer~~ Provide staff cover on the stand for agreed periods and
   act as interpreter (German and Russian).

Your/rate daily for this will be as/agreed previously, but we now agree to pay
your expenses in addition to your fee.

Please confirm your acceptance of this as soon as possible.
Can you recommend any hotels in Stuttgart and I will book
for all of us?

Yours sincerely

Sue Golding

<u>Cassette Tape</u> This has been a highly popular medium for many years. It is simple to handle and ideal for playing in the car.

RECORD

This traditional form of recording is slowly being phased out. However, it is still much sought after by collectors.

All our retail suppliers will receive the ~~A discount is available to all our~~ usual discount. ~~customers.~~ Telephone Susan Boyd for details.

Display stands and posters advertising the classical library are available on all stores to request.

draft catalogue entry

*double line spacing please
(extra between paras etc)*

BLOTTCO DESIGN

BlottCo is one of Britain's best-known design companies, specialising in marketing materials, corporate literature, exhibition stand design and packaging.

We have invested in the latest desk-top publishing packages and offer one of the fastest services anywhere.

Our customers include blue-chip corporations, TV companies, government departments and publishers in Britain and Europe.

Come and discuss your design needs on Stand 227.

Stand contact: Sue Golding

THE KEYBOARD

(change 'library' to 'collection' throughout)

Praxi Music ← (emphasise)

Our new classical library includes some of the most popular works ever written. (It is already proving to be a best seller.) The composers include:

Bach	Elgar
Beethoven	Greig
Chopin	Mendelssohn
Debussy	Offenbach

Puccini
Ravel
Tchaikovsky
Wagner

(type list in two columns) ↖

The library is available in all three recording media. ~~It is a perfect introduction to the best classics.~~

(change the following three paragraphs so that the style is as for <u>Cassette Tape</u> throughout)

COMPACT DISC

This is now by far the top seller for recorded music. Its many advantages include ease of use and the highest possible sound quality.

(rule box ~~leave space~~ at least 51mm high × 38mm wide (2" × 1½") here and in places marked ✱)

Assignment 3

The work is for Mrs Eccles, who works from home in Derby and writes articles for magazines and newsletters for local societies.

The work is:

- an extract for an article on Draycott village
- a letter complaining about a book.

You need:

- two sheets A4 plain paper
- an envelope (or label, if using word processor).

You should expect to take no more than an hour.

Re-type the following extract. Make amendments shown, and correct the circled words.

EXTRACT FROM THE HISTORY OF DRAYCOTT VILLAGE

A huge ~~exit~~ *exodus* of people from flooded fields to higher ground many

centuries ago gave Draycott its old English name. This was Dri-cote

or Draicott in the Domesday Book. It means dry place.

Draycott ~~remained~~ *stayed* just a small hamlet until the Industrial

Revolution. It then grew quickly as a centre (for) cotton doubling,

lace-making and ~~wool~~ *hosiery* trades in the ~~1800's~~ 1800s.

(Dracyott) spread over fields and meadows as more and more spinning

(mells) sprang up before 1900. It grew outwards from the South Street

(Street) - Market Street area. Many new homes were built for mill

workers. ~~There were small terraced houses for the mill workers but~~

~~the bosses had large semi-detached houses within easy access of~~

~~their workplace.~~

type as 2 words

Many listed buildings of unique style front on/to South Street. They

date from the 17th and 18th centuries.

~~Today~~ Industry provides (job) for about 700 people in the village. *Today, Draycott* ~~It~~

(was) mainly a commuter area for Derby and Nottingham.

THE KEYBOARD

Assignment 2

The work is for Praxi Music. The work is typical of text processing carried out by a secretary working for two executives, the Sales Manager and the Company Secretary.

The work is:

- quotation to Fair Price Music Store
- draft advertising material (two pages)
- details of promotional budgets (table)
- Financial Information Sheet
- letter to Mr G Roberts, Brittanic Hotel
- memo to Jim Clark.

You need:

- blank quotation form (at back of this book)
- 5 sheets A4 plain paper
- 1 Praxiteles letterhead
- 1 memo form
- 2 labels (approx 3" x 2").

Please complete the Quotation Form with these details:

To: Fair Price Music Store
272 High Street
ILFORD
Essex   IG1 7PG

	£
Compact disc display unit	59.50
Lightweight earphones	27.95
Cassette tape container	7.49
Anti-static cleaning cloth	5.99
Microphone (medium)	18.20
Microphone (small)	9.95

Delivery period 14-21 days from receipt of order

Contact name: Susan Boyd

53 Village Crescent
DERBY
DE21 6ZP

Sec: Check/Correct my
spelling — particularly
words I've circled

Mr
^Robert Hendry
Cannon Press ^Ltd
Cannon House
24 Maple St —
LEEK Staffs
S13 4WE

Dear Sir/s

Some time ago I ~~received~~ a copy of The Little School
Dictionary. It was a ~~free~~ gift with an order for a
~~referance~~ book. You can ~~see~~ therefore that I ~~just~~
~~loath~~ to complain too much about it.
^hesitate

When we came to use the ~~Dictionary~~ ^d we found that several
pages are blank. There are also some pages ~~with~~ which
/are
^poorly print~~ing~~ ^ed.

I am not sure who is ~~the~~ (responsable) ~~party~~ for ~~it~~ this, nor
to whom I should complain. I ordered the ~~referance~~
~~book~~ through a mail order company but am not
sure which one. Can you help?

The blank pages are 40-42 and 92-96. These are important
sections and the book is not really usable without
them. Poor printing is on pages 30, 36 and 43.
→ Despite a fairly thorough search ^locally, I have not
been ~~unable~~ to trace another copy to buy ~~locally~~.

Yours faithfully

Dilys Eccles

THE KEYBOARD

letter to

Stuart Diamond, Straight Line Design
(Please find his address from your
records (see Assignment 1, Section One))

Dear Stuart   'Kleenwater'

Lisa Menzies has given me ~~your name and suggested~~ the details of the/project
and has suggested
I contact you direct about the photographs you
need for the panels in the reception area, and
the three-dimensional models.

As far as the photographs are concerned, it
would seem best for us to set up two pumps
with filters in position, and to let you determine
how ~~best~~ we should mount them to best effect.
My colleague, Tim Desmet, suggests you ring
him and arrange to see the equipment one
day next week. You can then sort out between
you the best location.

The models are in course of production and Jim
Hallis is in charge. I think you and Jim
have worked ~~together~~ before. His first query
is whether or not the models are intended to be
cased, and if so, the dimensions you have in
mind. ~~Asty~~   Are the models to be base-mounted
or ~~sidemore~~ side-mounted against a vertical surface?
Perhaps you will talk to Jim when you phone Tim
and we can all get round the table sometime
in the near future.

We are all pleased you are ~~the~~ working with us
again. The Green World exhibition ~~was~~ was
a great success for us all. Yours sin. K Pete.

Assignment 4

In the first of a series of assignments set in a London clothes design company, Escadia Fashion Group Ltd, you are asked to type a letter from designer Vivien Peters and a fax from Alison Walton, the Customer Services manager. As with all the letters you will write for Escadia, the letter in this assignment should be presented on headed paper, a copy of which you will find at the end of the book. You should aim to produce the fax and letter within 30 minutes.

FAX   (Use plain paper)

To: Vivek Khatka (Production Manager)

From: Alison Walton (Customer Services Manager)

Dupion Strapless dress (Ref. L201 03 9X)

(type in capitals)   (one space here)   (no space here)

We have recently had several complaints from retailers and individual purchasers about the above garment.

It seems that in many cases the stitching attaching ~~holding~~ the bodice to the skirt is insufficiently strong to bear the extra tension which occurs when the garment is being worn, and is therefore subject to breaking and unfastening.

Could you notify your ~~~~ machinists of this problem before further dresses of this type are produced. ~~~~ We have already had to accept returned stock from several retailers!

THE KEYBOARD

Items in progress in Shop A, for which are all parts ~~withdrawn~~ withdrawn ~~~~ from ~~store~~ main store and maintained in Store 2.

Product Code	Finished Item Name	Specifications	
Mowers			
B31	Pup	12" cut	800W
B3/9	Kitten	14" cut	1000W
B42	Retriever	16" cut	1300 w
BT42	Labrador	16" cut	1500W
X42	Pony	16" cut	3.5 hp
X54	Bear	19" cut	4 hp
~~RS171~~	Strimmers		
RS171	Dove	Curved Shaft	16 cc
MX162	Starling	Straight Shaft	20 cc
Hedge Trimmers			
SHB386	Harty	14" Blade Brake	
SHB486	Bellow	26" Blade Brake	
B1X21	Bushbury	20" Slipping Clutch	
BTX31	Coster	26" Slipping Clutch	
Chainsaws			
285	Bambi	14" cut	1300 w
100	Paula	12" or 14" cut	33 cc
Shredders			
D1100	Chukka	25 mm capacity	
D1600H	Pinzer	30 mm capacity	
D1800Z	Butcher	30 mm capacity Pro	
D1800P	Jukky	30 mm capacity Pro	

Use small letters, one space after figure

When you've typed this, send it to Bernard Stokes in Materials Control for me. Write a covering memo enclosing it* Ask him to let me know if he wants quantities or any other information.

Thanks KP

* I'll sign it tomorrow.

159

Chic Modelling Agency
18 Gregory St
London   EC12 4UH

Use headed paper
+ prepare an envelope

Dear Sir / Madam

I wish to book eight female models
for a series of showings of our new Summer
collection beginning 15 [typist: insert next month] through
to 19 [next month.]!

We would like you to provide a shortlist
of about 20 girls who we shall invite to
our London offices ~~during the first two~~ at the beginning of
~~weeks of February for our designers, directors~~ next month for us
~~and sales managers~~ / to make a final
selection . [NEW PARAGRAPH] When drawing up your
shortlist, please bear in mind that we
shall be showing over 70 garments of all
types, including swimwear, and that this
year's collection has an 'exotic and
strongly ethnic flavour. This series of shows
will have audiences each day of 40-~~80~~ 50
people, including selected retailers and
representatives of the press.
I look forward to hearing from you soon
on availability of models etc!

Yours ffully
Vivien Peters
Designer

THE KEYBOARD

memo to

Jim B_____

Kevin P_____

You'll need extra copies – see below

Loreley's Garden Centre

Attached is copy of my letter to Trish Paten from which you'll see the shears have not yet arrived here for us to start our work on them. I know you promised Jean Hartley at Loreley's that we would have their order ready in double-quick time, but you can see we are now unlikely to be able to despatch everything as hoped.

I've got the ~~brass~~ other items on ~~their~~ Loreley's order well in progress, and I suggest you let Jean know that everything ~~but~~ the shears will be despatched in time / to arrive for their promotion weekend. Obviously, if ~~she~~ Trish does manage to get her factory people going, we'll send everything.

A copy of this is going to "Pat" Ghosal, so the Despatch Department will be alerted.

There'll also be a copy on Jayne's desk for when she comes back from holiday. She can ~~then~~ take over if all is not well by then. Also, I shall suggest Jayne tries to find an alternative supplier for the future, ~~an~~ although we have had good service from Spades & Forks in the past, and perhaps we shd give them the benefit of that and try them again.

Copies: ~~Mr~~ "Pat" Ghosal, Despatch
Jayne ~~Fisher~~ Fischer, Purchasing Office

Assignment 5

Here we begin a series of assignments about a Publishing
Company based in Nottingham called Mondori Publishing Ltd.
You have a memo and letter to type from the assistant editor,
Maria Beefley. As with all the letters you will write for Mondori,
the letter in this assignment should be presented on headed
paper, a copy of which you will find at the end of this book.
You should aim to produce an accurate memo and letter within
30 minutes.

MEMO

TO: Rosie Moreland, Publicity Officer
From: Maria Beefley
    Hollywood Lives } — *type in capitals at left margin*

This is to advise you that the publication date
of this title is being ~~changed~~ *pulled* back from next
Apr. to this Dec.

We're now aiming to catch the Christmas
market, so this book needs to go in the coming
autumn's catalogue and not the following spring's.
Let me know the deadline for catalogue copy as
soon as possible and I'll get working on it.

Keep informal style with apostrophes and type months in full.

When we spoke, you seemed to believe the shears were packed with the other goods. Indeed, your Delivery Note and Invoice refers to them. That is the reason for this letter: to confirm in writing that there is a shortfall.

In addition, you know we are very anxious to have the shears ~~in time~~ to carry out our own production processes in time for despatch to our customer. These processes take at least a half-day once we have arranged the machine capacity, and prepared the parts which you supply.

Whilst writing, I feel I should mention the other order we placed with you last month for a second consignment of these shears. The delivery date for that order is also now approaching. Is it possible for you to send the two lots together? The number of the second order ~~second~~ ~~number~~ is B.7821/JKP.

I will telephone you again tomorrow for an up-date.

Yours sincerely

Kevin Percy
Production Manager

copy to: Jim Bowles

Simone Marvell
18 Chappleton Road
Chichester
West Sussex
PO19 4DM

Please produce on headed paper & prepare an envelope too

Sec: we use informal style, so copy abbreviations such as I'm & so on

Dear Simone

Hollywood Lives

following
~~Further to~~ our telephone conversation this morning I'm writing to confirm that your typescript has gone into production. You will receive proofs on 12 July and will need to return them to me by 27 July. When I receive your corrections I will collate ~~them~~ with the independent proofreader's ~~copy editor~~ and, depending on how heavily they've been amended, we may see revised proofs. [new para] I hope this schedule fits in with your other commitments; let me know if it doesn't.

Yours sincerely

Maria Beesley { Assistant Editor

To end Section Two, here are four work assignments which are good practice for RSA Stage II exams and NVQ level 2 Business Administration document production.

Aim to complete each assignment, carefully checking your work, during a working period of about 2½ hours.

Assignment 1

This is an in-tray exercise in which you are producing work for Kevin Percy, Production Manager at Greenery Ltd.

This is the same firm as you worked for in Assignment 1, Section One, so you will already have used the Greenery Ltd letterhead.

The work here is:

- a letter to a manufacturer who is supplying us with parts which we use in some of the garden tools we produce
- a memo to a colleague who has asked for urgent delivery of tools to a customer
- a table with details of goods we keep in Store 2
- a memo sending the table to a colleague in Materials Control Department
- a letter to a designer who is preparing some exhibition materials for us.

letter to

Trish Paten
 Sales Division
Spades & Forks Ltd
Faversham Works
Rugby
CV23 0OSS

Dear Trish

OUR ORDER B.68241/JKP – URGENT

Sorry to have to contact you again, but following our telephone conversation today I have learned that the promised con-signment of garden shears has not, after all, arrived. I faxed your office immed. we realised they were not included with the delivery made by your van this afternoon.

Now you've mastered the basic skills you're ready for the office, and life gets much more interesting.

In this section, you move on from simply copying what was written and making simple amendments. You'll begin to use your professional judgement – just as you would at work – to:

▶ display work effectively and attractively

▶ spell words shortened in drafts

▶ correct words and sentences written (or previously typed) inaccurately. (In RSA Core Text Processing Skills Stage I and II exams, anything which you need to correct will be circled.)

You'll get used to remembering to:

▶ date all letters and memos

▶ use an enclosure mark when an attachment is mentioned.

Information and practice are provided for all of these. When you have finished Section One, you should be able to:

▶ copy type fluently and accurately

▶ tackle office type production work

▶ pass RSA exams
in Typewriting Skills Stage I or Word Processing Stage I.

Working Session 49

The two girls used to walk down the street each morning on their way to work. Tomorrow they will talk about the party.

There will be, however, much speculation about the causes of Mr Smith's problem. They will not be able to help you if you do not give them more details about it. Neither we nor they can be expected to do much without your help.

We are sure we can rely on you to take the necessary steps until further more permanent arrangements can be made.

Working Session 50

We have been dealing with your firm for many years and would not wish to consider taking our custom away from you. We do expect to receive some kind of explanation from you and an assurance that our statements will be very carefully checked in the future.

Working Session 53

MEMORANDUM

TO   Joan Kemp

FROM   [*Your name*], for Barry Feeney

[*Date of typing*]

PROOFREADING PROCEDURE CHART

Barry Feeney has asked me to send you this table in his absence. (Barry is away on business at the moment but will be returning in a week's time [*it would be preferable for you to give the date here*]).

The attached chart was drawn up as a result of your meeting with Barry Feeney last Tuesday. Could you:

1   check that the chart is exactly as you wanted

2   let me know of any amendments so that I can make them

3   photocopy it: a) enlarged to a size suitable for a wall
                            chart

                    b) reduced to a size suitable for a desk
                            reminder.

If you require any further information, do not hesitate to contact me.

[*Your initials*]

Don't rest on your laurels

Don't forget to use the Error Clinic on pages 201-7.

Work with a colleague

Ask someone – and it will be good if this can be someone who is also learning to type or to use a word processor – to work with you because:

▶ even when you've read and checked your work another person is often able to spot further errors

▶ a fresh eye may uncover misunderstandings or misreadings

▶ when you make errors a friend can help you see why you made them (mis-keyed a figure, mixed up keys or missed spaces).

Working sessions

The work for each session has:

▶ skills practice – with the chance to improve your use of punctuation and spelling as well as the keyboard

▶ underpinning knowledge – the things you need to know

▶ jobs typical of office work.

Assessment sessions

At the end of Section One there is some RSA exam material to give you an opportunity to test if you are ready for exams.

Machine check

Run a machine check to save time and give you confidence later on. Can you:

▶ justify the right margin automatically (word processors and some electronic typewriters)?

▶ print in bold type and use the underline (not all typewriters can print bold)?

▶ use the commands to end pages as asked in drafts (Page Break)?

Corrected versions

Working Session 42

Dear Sirs

With reference to your letter, please reserve accommodation for us on 10 of next month. We need three rooms in which to hold approximately 20 recruitment interviews. These are a result of our recent advertisements for staff in your area.

We acknowledge receipt of your account for last month and although we have one or two queries, we shall settle as soon as possible.

Yours faithfully

Working Session 44

Thank you very much for your telephone call today. We are indeed glad to hear that Dark Beauty has made such a swift improvement after the fall sustained during exercise last week. It is usually the case that recovery from such an injury is total. It leaves no lasting side effects. Nevertheless, I confirm that we will check during routine visits to ensure that good progress is maintained.

Working Session 46

GROUP MEETING ON THURSDAY

This Group frequently receives requests for help from prospective pet owners in search of healthy animals. It has therefore been suggested that we should produce a list of suitable pets. This would include brief details of animals available together with the breeder's name and telephone number.

Working Session 47

We invite you to our Reception at the Grand Hotel on Wednesday 28 February next at 5 pm.

The occasion is the 7th Anniversary of the opening of our Sheffield branch.

We look forward to meeting you and hope you will bring a guest.

Working Session 48

Dear Sirs

Thank you for your letter dated 6 November, from which we see that you will not be able to send us a machine to replace the one which was broken during transit.

We have looked through the catalogue you sent us. Please change our order to Item 684 on page 14. We note that the price of this machine is slightly more but hope you will not invoice us for the difference since the extra cost is beyond our control.

Warm-up: In and out

TYPE
```
a;sldkfjdksla;sldkfjdksla;sldkfjdksla;sldkfjdksla;
A;SLDKFJDKSLA;SLDKFJDKSLA;SLDKFJDKSLA;SLDKFJDKSLA;
a;sldkfjdksla;sldkfjdksla;sldkfjdksla;sldkfjdksla;
```

Copying practice: First fingers review

TYPE
```
fr4rfvf fr4rfvf frtrf frtrf fr5trf frt5trf fgt5tgf fgbvf
ju7ujmj ju7ujmj juyuj juyuj jy6yuj jhy6yhj juy6yuj jhnmj
fret breath bovine afrighted refrigerated vegetarian
favourites just jungle hymnal hypnotism jumping-bean
judgemental gymnastics regurgitate aggregation great
```

Punctuation practice:
Dash (between words) and hyphen (in words)

TYPE
The normal office hours are 9 – 5 Monday – Friday
with coffee breaks 10.30 – 10.45 and 3 – 3.15.
Representatives usually re-group each month and
at each meeting a post-dated sales record is
produced. The X-ray plate sales are always of
particular interest.

Spot the mistakes
Type the following, correcting the errors (there are six):

TYPE
```
We do not-nor do we intend to-have any large grees in
our garden. The fruit trees - apple, pear, cherry -
are all shrub or dwarf dwarf varieties which will not
grow highest than 3 foots.
```

Ask a colleague to check your copying and correcting work (see page 59 for corrected version).

File
File your paper copy of any work in which your colleague finds error(s), after you've marked it with a note of the cause of your mistake(s), if any.

Using a word processor?
You won't need to bring these paragraphs to screen again, so you can delete them from file/disk.

SKILLS PRACTICE

SECTION ONE

Letter, please, to J E Pensey, The Editor,
"Proper Culture" Magazine, James Publications Ltd
Broadway, GATESHEAD. Use Praxiteles Group letter-head.

As you're new to our house styles I've put notes
in on how we like MEASUREMENTS typed

Dear Miss Pensey

"Propogation" – Last month's issue, page 62

There were several misprints in the advertising
feature written by Molly Blaze. We checked the
copy sent to us for approval. These were
accurate and we still have them on file.
Nevertheless the errors appeared and they must
be rectified as soon and as effectively as
possible to avoid detrimental effects for
readers and, in turn, on sales of our
products.

For IVY (caps) the average temperature recommended
should read:

55-65°F (13-18°C)

> I know some people like
> to leave space after
> the figure but I prefer
> no space here

The directions for the cleaner mentioned should
be:

70 ml in 6 litres

> We do like a space
> before the measure,
> but please type
> 'litres' in full as
> shown (I know
> somepeople like
> to put 'l' in
> handwriting but
> I find that confusing)

// The flower screens are available
in heights up to 7'6"

> No space here

// The staging is also available in
the size 18" x 6'

> We do like a space here

Yours faithfully

> I don't know Miss Pensey so don't want to say
> 'sincerely' even though I've used her name

Barry Feeney

PRACTICE UNIT • MEASUREMENTS

WORKING SESSION 53

In the office (and in RSA exams) you have to remember to date all letters and memos. If documents are dated they can be easily found and identified, and people know if the information is up-to-date. In an RSA exam you will be penalised if you don't include the date.

Pick your style

The date is usually typed at the left margin. If you (or your employers) prefer it on the right, this is acceptable practice. The most usual way to present the date is:

> day, month, year – 24 January 1999

It is equally acceptable to use other styles, and in RSA exams no penalty will be incurred for style provided you make no errors in the proper date.

Note: Always set the document date apart from any other part of the document (eg address) by leaving space above and below it.

- If the word 'Date:' is pre-printed never type over that or any pre-printed dotted line.
- Never type the word 'Date' yourself before typing the date.

Whatever you (or your employers) decide, it is good practice to use the same style each time.

Remember: Dates can be very important.

- Make sure you date all letters and memos.
- If you're not told otherwise, it's wise to date all documents.
- Make sure the date is accurate and complete.

In-tray exercise

On the next two pages there is an in-tray exercise for Benson's Ltd. Benson's make display cabinets and therefore deal with a variety of businesses.

Step-by-step guide to accurate proofreading
Type the following table. File it where you can refer to it easily.

PROOFREADING PROCEDURE

STEP	PURPOSE	ACTION
1. Have whole page visible. Look at position of text	Is there space: - left and right - top and bottom - between items eg date/address - between paras?	NO? - Re-format (WP) OR Re-type after Step 5 YES? Go to Step 2
2. Compare with draft/file	Check: - names/address - attention line - subject/heading - marks, eg 'urgent'	Errors? Correct Now Accurate? Go to Step 3
3. View paragraphs one at a time. Scan	Any keying errors?	YES Correct Now Accurate? Go to Step 4
4. Read the paragraph "aloud" to yourself (mentally)	Can you "hear" any: - spelling errors - wrong words - bad punctuation	YES ~~Correct Now~~ Accurate? Go to Step 5
5. Compare with draft/file	Check facts: - dates, places - names, figures	Errors? Correct Now Accurate? Go to Step 6
6. Look at general appearance	Space now ok? Corrections acceptable? ~~NO?~~ ~~START AGAIN!~~	Yes Present for signature/despatch No? START AGAIN!

Sorry to leave you a complicated job. My typing (and ruling) is not very good, I'm afraid but I hope you can make a better job of this.

When it's finished send it with a memo to Joan Kemp. Remind her of our meeting last Tuesday. Ask her to check if the chart is as she wanted it. If she wants any amendments ask her to let you know & you can then change it. Ask Joan to photocopy it (a) enlarged to a size suitable for a wall chart and (b) reduced in size so it can be used as a desk reminder.

Thanks — Barry Feeney

File
When you are sure it's right, file your paper copy of these notes. There is an example of a suitable memo on page 155.

SECTION TWO

53 WORKING SESSION

Type this letter. Use plain paper and leave a top margin of at least 2 inches (5cm). This space is where the letterhead would go.

(Date)

D A Adamson Esq
42 Bell Street
LONDON SW17 4PQ

Dear Mr Adamson

We ~~are in receipt of~~ thank you for your letter dated 1st of ~~this month, and are~~ now able to tell you that our representative will be contacting you soon. We also apologise for the delay.

Mavis Parkwell is our new representative for your area. She joined our company only one month ago, and has been fully occupied since then on training and induction courses.

However, ~~Mary~~ Mavis has now been given all your details and we are sure she will be able to deal with your requests properly and without further undue delay.

We look forward to ~~/~~ receiving an order from you, and we hope this will be the start of a good working relationship between our companies.

Yours faithfully
BENSON'S LTD

James Johnson
Sales Department

Using a typewriter to complete pre-printed forms

At the back of the book on page 210 there is a remittance advice form (which you can cut out and photocopy) to use for the following practice:

Type three remittance advice forms:

To Cosby Coatings plc Derby Street WOLVERHAMPTON
WV22 8XD

£22.69   Inv No AB/142   Incl. VAT
49.91   JD/7   Part payment
28.71   c/463   —
Chq = 101.31   from Accounts Department

To G & H Middleways Ltd
Fortune Buildings Terry Lane LEEDS LS27 4JX
Cheque for £1177.22
Ref: Letter 20 Jan (this year)
Remarks: In full settlement of this matter.
B Purchasing Dept

To Fellowes, Bradley & Sons
37 Berry Landings
KIRKCALDY Fife KY16 22XF
Inv 2180   £17.21   Incl. £5 refund
2200   14.88
2202   194.62
2204   1110.00   See letter today
Cheque £1336.71

Check
When you're confident they're right, file your completed forms.

52
WORKING SESSION

Type a memo to Mavis Parkwell. Type headings as you see them if you do not have any memo forms.

MEMORANDUM

To M— P—   *Fill in gaps from details in the letter.*

From JJ   *Leave as initials. The writer hasn't left lines and gap*

D A Adamson 42 B— St— L—

I enclose a letter from Mr Adamson.

He runs an antiques business from his home, with several outlets in this area. This first order, which he wishes to discuss in detail, could lead to a series of other orders for a variety of our products.

All the best with this contact. It could be a good start for you.

Enc   *Type this as you see it. It's a reminder that another document is enclosed. Leave two or three lines clear after the message before you type Enc*

Don't forget to date all letters and memos

SECTION ONE

WORKING SESSION 27

Timed copying

Repeat the following until you can type it accurately within one minute (35 words a minute).

In the summer Cedric, residing in The Cedars in West Cheshire, invited his friend, Herbert Kent, with his wife, Betty, to stay at The Cedars for at least two months over the busy holiday period.

Copy the following notes for your file:

FORM-FILLING - <u>using pre-printed forms</u>

When you are asked to complete forms in the office, you will be supplied with the information which is to be entered on the form.

Remember! *use capitals*

-- look at the form to see what headings ~~are~~ *have* to be completed.
-- on the information you are given, put a cross by each of the details for which there is a *seperate* heading on the form.
align with line above
This is important because the details may not be given to you in the same way, or in the same sequence, as the headings on the form.

<u>Using a typewriter</u>

Always be careful to avoid typing over any of the printing.

<u>Using a word processor</u>

You will not normally be asked to fill in a pre-printed form using a word processor. If there is a single form to be completed you will probably use a typewriter. If a form is in frequent use a common practice is for it to be stored in the word processing system for you to recall to screen and enter the details at pre-set points.

Check

When you're sure they're right, file your paper copy of these notes. Word processor users will not need to bring this material back to screen.

Using a word processor?
You may omit the Workshop for this session. Move on to Working Session 53.

Warm-up: In and out on qwerty line

TYPE
```
qpwoeirutyrueiwoeirueiwoq
pwoeirutyrueiwoqpwoeirutyruei
QPWOEIRUTYRUEIWOEIRUEIWOQP
WOEIRUTYRUEIWOQPWOEIRUTYTUEI
qpwoeirutyrueiwoeirueiwoq
pwoeirutyrueiwoqpwoeirutyruei
```

Copying practice: Right hand review

TYPE
```
I know you will not look too long at my jumping score,
about which I am particularly humble. How do you keep up
your own score so consistently? My most important
pointers so far are from the book "Looking Up" by Jimmy
Johns.
```

Punctuation practice: Quotation

TYPE
```
"Did you want to see me today?" asked Joan.  "No, thank
you, but I would like to have a chat tomorrow before you
go to meet David at 'Channings' in the afternoon" replied
Frank.
```

Spot the mistakes

Re-type the following, correcting the errors (there are five):

TYPE
```
"For the triumph of evill it is only neccesary that
good men do nothing." was itEdmund Burke who said
that.
```

Ask a colleague to check your copying and correcting work (see page 62 for corrected version).
File your work.

Retrieve your work from Working Session 27. Re-type any work in which uncorrected errors were found. If you were accurate, re-type the drills and try to increase your speed.

> ### *Corrected version – Working Session 27*
> We do not – nor do we intend to – have any large trees in our garden. The fruit trees – apple, pear, cherry – are all shrub or dwarf varieties which will not grow higher than 3 feet.

SKILLS PRACTICE

SECTION ONE

Correcting other people's errors

Type the following, correcting all the circled errors and making the changes asked for:

Despite

Outline Proposals for ~~Extention~~ of Branch Activities *Type this line in capitals*

Use double linespacing throughout   *bouyant*

~~In~~ the current economic climate the Group has been, and still is, incurring loss of business. The Annual Report does not necessarily reflect this loss; not until we look ~~carefulley~~ at the sales figures for our competitors and the Gross National Product Analysis does the shortfall become apparent.

From a recent survey it becomes clear that we must not be complacent. One of the ~~biggest~~ advantages enjoyed by our largest competitors is the ~~High Street~~ outlet. *in local shopping parades.* Customers have repeatedly cited one of the biggest advantages ~~and attractions~~ of those rivals as the availability of ~~their~~ services without the need ~~for~~ *to* travel to the city.

In the past we have been determined to avoid the additional costs of local branch business. It may now be time for this policy ~~should change.~~ *to be reconsidered.*

A feasibility study has now been launched. It will look first at two towns in the South West of England. The study will be carried out *during* ~~over a period of twelvemonths~~ and will target the following queries: *the next financial year*

-- *likely setting up* costs of one branch in the town

-- amount of business available ~~fixed~~ for one other branch in the suburbs *line up with line above*

-- *likely setting up* costs of one ~~other~~ branch in the suburbs *extra* (if business justifies)

-- possibility of increasing our share of business in the town

-- possibility of ~~enhancing~~ *increasing* the amount of business for our type of service within the town

-- availability of property to rent/to ~~perchase~~

Check

It is up to you to make sure your work is accurate. This doesn't mean you have to be the only person to check your work. In a job you should ask colleagues to double check to make sure errors are not missed.

SECTION TWO

Some of the practice earlier in this book has included handwritten alterations, crossing through word(s) you should leave out and using the sign ╱ to show you should type in something extra.

Most people in offices use these and other signs as messages to you to make amendments.

Re-type the following, making all the amendments required. You should be able to interpret all the signs.

There is a worked example on the next page for you to check that you do understand the amendment signs.

Straighten the left margin

The cleaning service offers the most comprehensive
Our

techniques normally available only to industrial

and commercial customers and not to private

householders.

Prices are very competitive.

Exports bring to your home the equipment and materials

which enable quick, thorough and economical cleaning

of your carpets, curtains and furniture. All
fully
degreasing materials are tested before application to

your upholstery. and You are fully insured against:

fire
breakages
water damages

which might occur through breakdown of machinery.
t
We guarantee the safely of your valuable ornaments.

We guarantee your satisfaction. You will be convinced

when you see again the brightness brought back to your

furniture. Our representative will give you a fully

comprehensive quotation.

Timed copying

Try to copy this, including all the capitals and spaced capitals, within three minutes:

```
Headings can be emphasised by typing them in CAPITALS and in
S P A C E D   C A P I T A L S.  We must leave more than one space
to show the end of each word in spaced capitals.

If spaced letters are used next to words without spaces, it is
better to leave extra space  B E F O R E  and  A F T E R  the
spaced words.

We can also use capitals for the first letter in each word to
highlight items in, say, draft advertisements: This Will Call
Attention To The Words And Provides Another Option When Other
Types Of Capitalisation Have Been Used.
```

Linespacing

Before typing the next exercise, find out from your manual or guide how to regulate linespacing. Here, you'll use double line spacing, generally used on draft documents to allow room for the author to make alterations.

Set your machine for double linespacing and a typing line of 65. Try to type this piece of work accurately within three minutes.

You'll have to leave at least one extra line without any typing on it between the paragraphs so that the start of each new paragraph can be clearly seen. Word processor users can tap 'return' once for this extra line. Typewriter users: if your linespace regulator is on '2' you may have to put in the extra line manually.

```
Thank you for your letter dated 13 of last month.  I regret the

delay in replying.  This has been because I was on holiday.  I am

going away on business next month and am visiting Scotland.  As I

shall be travelling by road it occurs to me that I could stop in

Harrogate on the way home.  Would Thursday 2 be convenient?

Perhaps you would drop me a line before then.  If your letter

arrives after I leave for Scotland, a message can be sent to me.
```

Check

Did you copy accurately – including all capitals and spaces – in the suggested times? If so, you are typing at about 30 words a minute.

If not, type again the exercises in which you made mistakes. When they're right, move on.

PRACTICE UNIT

SECTION TWO

Our cleaning service offers the most comprehensive techniques available normally only to industrial and commercial customers and not to private householders.

Prices are very competitive.

Experts bring to your home the equipment and materials which enable quick, thorough and economical cleaning of your carpets, curtains and furniture. All degreasing materials are fully tested before application to your upholstery. You are fully insured against:

      breakages
      water damages
      fire

which might occur through breakdown of machinery. We guarantee the safety of your valuable ornaments. We guarantee your satisfaction.

You will be convinced when you see the brightness brought back to your furniture.

Our representative will give you a fully comprehensive quotation.

UNDERPINNING KNOWLEDGE • WORKED EXAMPLE

SECTION ONE

Ruled tables

There are two tables to be typed and ruled in this workshop. Allow yourself about 35 minutes for each one; this time should include sorting. You can practise your count/number/type/count routine.

Discount Sales

Please re-arrange items in page order, starting 25 and to 82

Abbreviation for centilitre. Small letters, no space

	Sizes available *		Page
Whisky	70 cl	150 cl	79
Sparkling Wine	75 cl	~~1 litre~~	77
Vodka	75 cl	1 litre	80
Bordeaux	70 cl	75 cl	25
Beaujolais	75 cl	150cl	29
Armagnac	35cl	70cl	78
Bitters	10 cl	15cl	82
Gin	75 cl	140 cl	80
Champagne	75cl	Magnum	75-76

* Other sizes available - details on request

When you type this second table, as well as re-arranging the items into alphabetical order of authors, you have to modify the layout so that the list of book titles becomes the first column.

FURTHER TITLES

Please type in alphabetical order of authors. Type Titles as first column.

Author	Title	Publisher	Year
Fleming G H	The Small English Garden	Joseph	1971
Gaute R H	History of the west Ridings	York Press	1948*
Allen W G	Scottish Relics	Gould plc	1987
Bench VR	Herb Gardens	Boult + Co	1980
Hardy SE	Country Houses in Yorkshire	Heinemann	1984
Davis JA	Walks in Wessex	Mandy Press	1940
Waygood M	The Ramblers' Way	Bendower	1985
Cheylesmore P G	Post-War Coventry	Barrow Press	1960**

* Out of print 1988

** Out of print 1992

WORKSHOP 10

Warm-up: Phrase drill

TYPE Dear Sirs, Dear Madam; Thank you for your letter;
Yours faithfully;
I shall be glad if you will; Please give this your
urgent attention;
We look forward to hearing from you; We are in receipt
of your note;
This is to confirm our telephone conversation; Yours
sincerely.

Copying practice: Mainly third and fourth fingers

TYPE As soon as we are able to look for extra people we
shall approach all of our agents who are in the
Western Areas. Please pass word to all possible people
who are new and/or staff who saw the news in "News
Extra".

Copying accurate spelling

TYPE We cannot guarantee your business accommodation will be
available if your accounts are not settled immediately.
We can exercise some discretion but in the light of our
experience with government departments we feel we must
make some amendment to the contract.

Spot the mistakes

Re-type the following, correcting the errors (there are nine):

TYPE Anyone in busness today must be aware of goverment
regulations witch we believe can determine how
successfull a company may be at the end of it's first
year.

We cannot anticipate or guarrantee the ammount of support
which will be needed; nor how promptly cash will be
recieved through customers settling account's monthly.

Check

Ask a colleague to check your copying and correcting work
(see page 66 for corrected version).
File your work.

> **Corrected version – Working Session 28**
> "For the triumph of evil it is only necessary that good men do
> nothing." Was it Edmund Burke who said that?

SECTION ONE

WORKING SESSION 29

Ruling using your machine

Many typewriters and word processors have a key or function to rule lines down the page, as well as lines across the page.

Try to set up tab stops and type and print this table in less than ten minutes. Use underline to rule horizontal lines. If your machine doesn't have a vertical ruler, rule down the sides and between the columns with black pen or ball-point after taking the typed/printed sheet out of the machine.

Customer	Query	Dealt with by	
		(Leave only one line clear here)	
	(Leave one clear line)	Name	Date
			(Leave more space before ruling)
PLD	Delivery	B Hardy	June 6
Verity's	Price	M T Head	May 2
Lamberts	Delivery	B T Bell	June 30
Fenwicks	Order details	B Hardy	May 17
Mastersons	Damage	L C Temms	June 14
Martins	Colour	U R Good	June

Check

It's important to be able to work at a reasonable rate of production, so if you did finish accurate work, attractively ruled, in ten minutes this is excellent. Remember, though, an employer would far rather you produced work which is a credit to the firm than for you to send out poor work done quickly.

Spot the mistakes

Type and correct the errors (there are seven):

We have been dealing with your firm for many year and would not wish to consider tasking our custom away from your. We do expect to receipt some kind of explannation from you and an assurance that our statements will be very careful checked in the future.

Check

Remember, your word processor Spellchecker will not help you with several of the errors. There's a corrected version on page 155 for you to check.

SECTION TWO

When people prepare drafts in handwriting they often take short-cuts such as:

- writing only part of an item, for example an address; you worked with some examples of this in Working Session 27.
- shortening words.

Copying from handwriting is part of the work in almost all offices (and in RSA exams). You can prepare yourself to produce accurate copy quickly by making sure you know how to spell words most commonly used and abbreviated. For those words you can't always remember, keep a pocket dictionary with you as one of the tools of your trade.

In-tray exercise

On this page and the next there is an in-tray exercise of a memo and a letter. It includes abbreviated words. Check on page 65 how to spell these correctly.

MEMORANDUM

To   Lisa Bayles
From   Barry Hughes

Use today's date

I attach a letter from Mr Belling in Edinburgh.

manufacturers
Rachel will write to him. We may be able to contact (mfrs) thro' him. Rachel wl suggest Jack Peele handles any response.

catalogue
On the matter of the cat., I know you wl wish to deal with the printers. Perhaps it's a blessing we made only a temp. arrangement with Gentry & Co. However, until we have suff. work to (gntee) approx. six months' work I feel we must keep our options open.
guarantee

Eric

WORKING SESSION 29

<u>Other Pets</u>

Birds and small mammals should be in secure cages. They suffer less disorientation if cages are kept covered.

<u>Safety</u>

Make sure your pet is always fully protected. ✳ Move this line to run on after 'diseases' on page 1 and underline it.

Any pet carried in a car must be confined or secured in such a way that it cannot interfere with safe driving. If you transport your dog by car, take extra care in the car park, where there will necessarily be other animals.

page 3 starts here

AT THE SURGERY
Please keep all dogs on leashes in the waiting room.
Large dogs may respond badly to the presence of other animals.
It is wiser to ask a relative or friend to sit in the waiting room whilst you wait outside with your pet until the vet is ready for you.

Cats, birds and other pets should remain in fully secured containers.

REMEMBER:
Repeat lines from page 1

Double linespacing and inset these lines 10 spaces from left margin

Check

Ask someone else to read your work, comparing it with the final version from which you have typed, to see whether you have made all the corrections accurately, and made no other mistakes.

When you're sure it's right, file your paper copy to give you practice in filing. Word processor users will not need to bring this work back to screen again.

SECTION TWO

BENSON'S LTD
Adam Street
LONDON WC2N 6EZ

(Today's date)

Mr
J D Belling
28 Fillonghby Ave.
Belton Park
EDINBURGH
EH9 8XT

Dr. Sir

We have recd. yr letter ~p~ with ref. to discrepancies in descriptions on various pages in our cat., and thank you for the info. you give.

Our Publicity Manager is taking immed. action to put things right, and we are asking our printers for a guarantee that this exp. wl not be repeated.

In the meantime, ~ple~ may we take this opp. to ask if, as part of your agency work, you dev. contacts w. mfrs. of misc. engineering tools? We place adverts. in sep. publications but def. feel that cos. who are refd. directly to us provide greater opps. for meeting the very high requirements of our member cos. If you can recom. anyone to us, perhaps you will telephone Jack Peele, our officer resp. for new developments.

We apologise for any incon. caused by our cat. descriptions, and again thank you for your attention.

Yrs ffly

Rachel Downey
Customer Relations

WORKING
SESSION
29

Long documents

Using a word processor?

Find and bring back to screen the draft document you filed in Working Session 47 headed 'Visiting the Vet'. Add to it and make the changes shown in the final version:

Using a typewriter?

You did not prepare the first draft. Type the final version of the article as follows:

Type the heading LEAFLET at top left of each page, and number pages 2 and 3 at the bottom

DRAFT

VISITING THE VET ← Centre this line

It is the responsibility of all owners to ensure that their pets are given no opportunity to attack other patients and are protected from other animals.

Several visits will be needed during your pet's lifetime. Animals need annual innoculations to prevent spread of infectious diseases ✳ ← see overleaf

Repeat these lines at end of last page after REMEMBER

page 2 starts here

TRANSPORTING YOUR PET

Dogs

Dogs can often be walked to the surgery. Always keep your dog on a leash in built-up areas.

Cats

Please change 'containers' to 'carriers' throughout

Cats are best transported in specially designed containers. A small blanket on the floor of the carrier gives comfort and reassurance to your pet. Cheap temporary containers, made of cardboard, can be bought. Do check that the carrier is securely fastened. Make sure straps are in good condition. Nervous cats can escape thro' a surprisingly small space.

Check your spellings from the complete list of words you may need to spell out in RSA exams – see below. The shortened versions which may be used in exams are in columns 1 and 3.

accom	accommodation	opp(s)	opportunity/ies
a/c(s)	account(s)	org	organisation
ack	acknowledge	p/t	part time
advert(s)	advertisement(s)	poss	possible
altho'	although	rec(s)	receipt(s)
appt(s)	appointment(s)	rec	receive
approx	approximate/ly	recd	received
asap	as soon as possible	recom	recommend
bel	believe	ref(s)	reference(s)
bus	business	refd	referred
cat(s)	catalogue(s)	resp	responsible
cttee(s)	committee(s)	sec(s)	secretary/ies
co(s)	company/ies	sep	separate
def	definite/ly	sig(s)	signature(s)
dev	develop	suff	sufficient
ex	exercise	temp	temporary
exp(s)	expense(s)	thro'	through
exp	experience		
f/t	full time	sh	shall
gov(s)	government(s)	shd	should
gntee(s)	guarantee(s)	wh	which
hrs	hours	wd	would
immed	immediate/ly	w	with
incon	inconvenient/ence	wl	will
info	information	yr(s)	year(s)
mfr(s)	manufacturer(s)	yr(s)	your(s)
misc	miscellaneous	dr	dear
necy	necessary		

days of the week (e.g. Thurs, Fri)
months of the year (e.g. Jan, Feb)
words in address (e.g. Cres, Dr)
complimentary closes (e.g. ffly)

(N.B. Until Stage II, full stops are included to indicate abbreviations.)

Correcting other people's mistakes

Type the following, correcting errors in spelling, grammar and punctuation:

The two ~~gitale~~ girls
~~Sharon~~/used to walks down the street each morning ~~ou~~ ~~her~~ way to work. Tomorrow they will talked about the party.

There will be, however, much speculation about the causes of Mr Smiths problems. They will not, be able to help you; if you do neither not give them more; details about it. ^ we nor they can be expected to do much without your help.

We are sure we can rely on you to take the neccessary steps untill further more permenent arangments can be made.

Check

There's a corrected version on page 155 so you can check whether you spotted all the mistakes.

Timed copying

Aim to type this within two minutes:

Today's official minimum for new dwellings is 4" of loft insulation, but 6" is a better investment.

How do we arrive at 6"? A standard method is to add the cost of installation to the likely cost of heat loss.

Most joists are made of 4" timber, so if your insulation does not come to the top of them it needs topping up.

Check

Accurate first time and finished in two minutes?
Excellent. You're typing at about 35 words a minute – well on target for this Section.

Made mistakes?
Try again. Type more slowly and get it right. It's better to be slightly slower and accurate than to rush and make mistakes.

Errors can be:

Typographical — errors in work previously typed, eg no space between words, uneven margin, wrong letters, overtyping (typewriters), handwritten letters as corrections.

Grammatical — these include errors of agreement, eg "The matter are . . ." (instead of "The matter is . . ."), and errors of tense, eg "Yesterday we look at new office furniture."

Punctuation — including mis-use or omission of apostrophes, eg "The three cat's food . . ." or "We dont . . ." (instead of "The three cats' food . . ." or "We don't . . .").

Re-type the following, then check yourself with the worked examples on page 93.

TYPE

There are a lot of companies ~~who~~, *which* these days, (does) not have the computer facilities to carry out all of their own data processing, because they prefer to use the services of a computer bureau.

A bureau can build up sufficient custom to justify the purchase of larger and more (xpensive) machines than an individual company may be able to install. (this,) of course, enables the bureau to complete (it's) work very quickly, as well as undertaking jobs requiring very sophisticated (program's) and hardware.

When we (discussed) the matter of the new contract at our meeting tomorrow we mu(st,) make sure Clauses 17 and 19 (does) not take up too much time. Clause 21 is concerned with the individual office (workers) access to further training and mu(st,) therefore be decided upon at (tomorrows) meeting.

Everything in the contract is significant in some respect, but as next week's staff council meeting is on the subject of training it will be more than useful to have a decision from (officer's) on (Cluase) 21.

> **Corrected version – Working Session 29**
> Anyone in business today must be aware of government regulations which we believe can determine how successful a company may be at the end of its first year.
>
> We cannot anticipate or guarantee the amount of support which will be needed; nor how promptly cash will be received through customers settling accounts monthly.

SECTION ONE

WORKING SESSION 30

~~can give the opportunity for additional display space~~. Demonstration space can usually be made available if booked in advance. Such space is normally ~~free~~. Current charges for stalls are shown on the enclosed booking form.

Also enclosed is a leaflet giving details of booking conditions. [All new exhibitors are asked to complete the sep form giving (their) full description of (a) craft. The form should then be sent to us as soon as possible. These will be returned ~~with a~~ promptly

at the co's exp.

~~decision as to whether or not the craft is acceptable for our fairs.~~ As you will realise, this simple measure helps to maintain the standard of our fairs and safeguards quality crafts.

hope to hear from you in the near future and
We / wish you success with your craft venture.

Yrs sinc
PRAXITELES GROUP

, together w either photographs or samples of the exhibitor's work

Craft Fair Promoter

provided demonstration actually takes place throughout the fair

Check

Ask someone else to read your letter. Have you:
- accurately spelled out the words shortened by the writer?
- made all the changes asked for?

Accurate?

When you've made any necessary corrections, file your work.

Using a word processor?

You won't need to bring this letter back to screen.

In this assignment you are typing work for David Selcombe, who is a journalist working for a TV company. Mr Selcombe works from his home in Blackheath. The work here is:

- a letter from Mr Selcombe to an acquaintance, Martin Keane
- to re-type the first page of an article Mr Selcombe is writing.

Aim to type an accurate letter, envelope and article within an hour.

This assignment is very similar to an RSA exam in CORE TEXT PROCESSING SKILLS. In the exam, you have an hour to complete all the work. If you use a word processor, you can prepare a label, or use a typewriter for the envelope. You can, of course, use a typewriter for all of the work.

There are worked examples on page 93 and page 94.

The Links
27 Marloux Cresc.
BLACKHEATH
London
SE3 6BT

Type this letter on plain A4 paper

Mr M Keane
The Watch House
19 Rangefield Dr.
MILTON KEYNES
MK12 9PR

Dear Martin

I was very pleased to rec. your letter. The delay in replying is because I was away on a bus. trip to Holland.

It is not always easy to find suitable accom. at short notice. Lucy and I are glad to hear that you are now quite settled in your new home.

The co. has renewed my contract for a further period of two years. We are very happy to know that we are def. settled here for that period of time.

We sh. look forward to seeing you again soon. We have made our spare room into an office. Lucy is acting as my sec. as most of my work is now done at home.

Yours sncly.

David

Type an envelope for Martin's letter (or a label)

67

ASSIGNMENT

31

SECTION ONE

URGENT

Mrs N Stevens
32 Rington Rd
Sawbridgeworth
Hertfordshire
CM21 9JH

(number the 2nd page)

Dr Mrs Stevens

~~PRAXITELES~~ CRAFT FAIRS

Thank you for your enquiry about craft fair promotions. You wl see from the attached cat that many of our venues are already fully booked.

There are vacancies for certain crafts at events printed in red on the schedule. Please let me know immed if you wd like to book any of these vacancies. ~~It is not feasible at present to specify which crafts are "missing" from any particular venue as exhibitors constantly produce fresh and original ideas.~~ I shd explain that we try to keep duplication of crafts to a minimum at our fairs. This allows better opps for craftspeople. It also means that a wider range of crafts can be represented. This def makes the event more attractive to visitors.

All our fairs are well signposted. Local dwellings are leafleted well in advance and we also distribute adverts in the town centre on the day of the event.

Only items made by the exhibitor or a close family member may be offered for sale at our fairs. This policy is strictly maintained at all venues. ~~Our representative is expected to visit each stall during the course of the fair to check that this is so.~~

✓ The ~~basic table~~ ~~standard stall~~ comprises a 6ft table and 2 chairs. There is normally a choice of centre or side stalls. ~~A side stall is normally backed by a wall which, at some venues,~~

If you are (thinkong) of going into franchising, do not make a hasty decision. Stop and think. Check thoroughly first. Ensure that you get the right guidance.

The buyer of a franchise buys the rights to a whole business package. A lump sum must be paid, plus a franchise fee, plus royalties.

The seller (provide) a famous name ~~also~~ and its reputation. Also included in the package is the product or service, plus the know-how to ensure the success of the new outlet. There is no need for the franchisee to be an expert in the particular business chosen. You simply hire the necessary experienced staff.

To be successful you (neeed) resources, both financial and personal. You must have ambition and be prepared to work hard.

You should check the data about any offer and the track record of the company ~~offering~~ selling the franchise.

Over the next few years it (are) expected that the annual turnover of franchises will be more than doubled.

ASSIGNMENT

SECTION ONE

WORKING SESSION 31

Filling gaps

Sometimes handwriting is hard to read or an outline is missing in shorthand and you have to work out what the missing word is. Type the following to practise filling gaps; the number of dots is the number of letters in the missing words.

Dear Sirs

..... you for your letter. ...... 6 November, from which we ... that you will not be .... to send us a machine .. replace the one which ... broken during transit.

// We have ...... through the catalogue you .... us. Please change our ..... to Item 684 on page 14. .. note that the price .. this machine is slightly .... but hope you will ... invoice us for the .... since the extra cost is ...... our control.

Check

Now ask a friend to read the above and suggest words to fill the gaps to see if you agree on the missing words. There's a corrected version on page 154. You might be able to use other words, with a different number of letters, but which also make good sense.

Continuation sheets

Type the following notes about continuation sheets. File for easy

CONTINUATION SHEETS

Long letters

Only one sheet of headed notepaper shd be used. After the first page, use plain paper. // It is usual to start numbering pages after the first page.

Good Practice

It's a good idea to type on all continuation sheets:
- page number
- date
- name of person or firm to whom the letter is addressed

use double linespacing and inset about 1" from left margin

This is useful if, at some future time, the top page is separated from the others.

Most people type these details at the left margin, starting about one inch from the top edge of the paper.

Warm-up: Alphabet

TYPE abcdefghijklmnopqrstuvwxyz ABCDEFGHIJKLMNOPQRSTUVWXYZ

Copying practice: Left hand review

TYPE Save Electricity! Dress for the weather! Be sensible!
We are always attempting to save money in every way we
can. We should extend this to finding ways in which the
environmental cause can be assisted at the same time as
we are watching out for expenses.

Punctuation practice: Brackets

TYPE We are not able (not yet, anyway) to tell you why the lipsticks you mention (Holly, Peach and Apricot) were damaged on receipt. They are items (A) (F) and (P) in our list.

Are there any other matters you wish to take up with the manufacturers (Pan & Cake Ltd)? We will be in contact with them soon (but not before 26th).

Spot the mistakes

Re-type the following, correcting the errors (there are six):

TYPE We do not need your help (although we are greatful for
the offer) in the matter currantly outstanding. if
you are able to give us us some assistance in the
future - particularly with our socail work - we shall
be pleased.

Checking

Ask a colleague to check your copying and correcting work
(see page 72 for corrected version).

File any work in which your colleague finds error(s), after you've
marked it with a note of the cause of your mistake(s).

Retrieve your work from the last Working Session. Re-type any
work in which uncorrected errors were found.

Preparing draft documents
Using a word processor?
You need not print this first draft. When it's keyed in, save it ready to bring back to screen when needed.

Check 'Page Break' in your manual/guide so that you can enter the right print instructions to print the three pages when needed.

Using a typewriter?
You can omit this first draft stage. Move to Working Session 49 after you've completed Working Session 48.

```
VISITING THE VET

It is the responsibility of all owners to ensure that their pets
are given no opportunity to attack other patients and are
protected from other animals.
```

PAGE BREAK

```
TRANSPORTING YOUR PET

Dogs

Dogs can often be walked to the surgery.

Cats

Cats are best transported in specially designed containers.  A
small blanket on the floor of the carrier gives comfort
and reassurance to your pet.  Cheap temporary containers, made of
card board can be bought.

Other Pets

Birds and small mammals should be in secure cages.

Safety

Make sure your pet is always fully protected.
```

PAGE BREAK

```
AT THE SURGERY

Large dogs may respond badly to the presence of other animals.
It is wiser to ask a relative or friend to sit in the waitingroom
whilst you wait outside with your pet until the vet is ready for
you.

Cats, birds and other pets should remain in fully secured
containers.
```

SECTION TWO

In the office (and in RSA exams) you have to show there is an enclosure and 'Enc' won't be written in the draft for you to copy.

When you notice an enclosure is mentioned within the wording, make yourself a reminder, such as a pencil note at the foot of the draft.

Leave a few lines clear after the message in a memo and after the signature block in a letter before you type 'Enc' at the margin.

Some companies have a different way of doing this: they may stick on a stamp printed with 'Enc' or they may ask you to type a few dots or dashes in the margin where enclosures are mentioned.

In RSA exams, no penalties will be incurred for the style, provided you do notice when an enclosure is mentioned, and show this clearly.

Type the following memo, remembering to date it and to show there is an enclosure:

MEMORANDUM

To Fred Archer

From Joe Jenkins

D A Adamson Esq   (Type his address here. You've got it in your file from Working Session 27)

This could be a very good contact.

I have sent his letter to Mavis Parkwell asking her to get in touch.

I now enclose a sample of ~~some~~ Mr Adamson's work. You will see how good it is, but also how many of our products could be used by him in this type of work.

Is there anything special you think we should tell or pass to Mavis to improve her prospects of securing a good order?

Completing draft article

Find from your file: Article headed 'GROUP MEETING ON THURSDAY' which you started and filed in Working Session 46.

Using a word processor?
Bring the article back to screen.

Using a typewriter?
Put the article back into your typewriter. If your typewriter cannot justify automatically, type with a ragged right margin.

Type/print one copy with justified right margin.
Use a typing line of 50 (eg margins at 20 and 70)
Make changes and add paragraphs as shown.

GROUP MEETING ON THURSDAY ← Please give date for Thurs. of next week

This Group frequently receives requests for help from prospective pet owners in search of healthy animals. It has therefore been suggested that we should produce a list of suitable pets. This would include brief details of animals available together with the breeder's name and telephone number.

first   agreed
Animals should be examined by one of us. An/fee would be payable by breeders.

                    could
The current list be displayed at the surgery.
                              also
Potential purchasers could/collect a free copy from the duty receptionist. at the surgery.

Please consider the feasibility of this before the
meeting on give date from above.

BENSON'S LTD
Adam Street
London WC2N 6EZ

Miss J Stokes
14 Remming Way
Penn
Wolverhampton
WV4 88ST

Dear Jenny

It has come to my notice that you have not yet seen a copy of our new leaflet covering our "Petal" range of display cabinets. A copy is enclosed and as usual no doubt you will order extra copies from Publications Office if you think it will be of interest to your contacts.

Mavis tells me you are enjoying your work with us. That's good news, and I look forward to hearing more about it at the regional meeting next month.

Best wishes
Yours sincerely
Brenda Warbrick
Sales Department

Spelling

Type the following, correcting any spelling errors:

We invite you to our Reception at the Grand Hotel on Wendesday 28 Febuary next at 5 pm.

The ocassion is the 7th Aniversary of the opening of our Sheffeild branch.

We look forward to meeting you and hope you will bring a gesst.

There's a corrected version on page 154 for you to check.

Setting-up

Try to set tab stops and type/print the table in no more than 25 minutes:

Ruling by hand ◄—[Type in Spaced capitals]	
DO	WHY
Use a flat, clean ruler	Old ink stains leave stains on your work
Use a straight ruler	Wooden ones may warp
Experiment with pens*	You want one that - produces fine lines - does not blot**
Have a soft lead pencil handy***	You can rule first in pencil to make sure lines are straight and in the right place before ruling in pen
Keep a soft eraser	To remove pencil ~~lines~~ marks

(Leave 3 clear lines here)

* Use the colour (usually black) which matches your typing/print ~~ribbon~~

** Some ballpoints leave sticky blobs where you start/stop ruling

*** 2B with a fine point

Check

Make sure your work is accurate. Before you file your copy look at it carefully. Could you have left more or less space anywhere to have improved it? If so, make a note to help you improve your display in future.

Warm-up: Figures

TYPE 1234567890 11 12 13 14 15 16 17 18 19 20 0987654321
14 April 1993 25 May 1994 3 June 1995 4 July 1996

Copying practice: Double letter review

TYPE better butter opportunity appointment difficulty
challenge freedom
pillion saddle dinner supper spoon summer beginning
blubber cheese

Dolly's buffet will be in three weeks' time. Billy's
wedding will be seventeen days later. These occasions
will be opportunities for us to wish them happiness at
the beginning of Dolly's different career and Billy's
marriage.

Punctuation practice: Apostrophe

TYPE *It's part of this company's policy that employees' records are available for inspection at any time (during normal working hours). Each individual's file will be identified by number.*

Supervisors'
Entries to each file will be signed when agreed by both parties. This note will be confirmed in four days' time.

Spot the mistakes

Re-type the following, correcting the errors (there are six):

TYPE It's not for us to complain about other people's failures
in the dance championship (there failure may improve
our opportunities). Nevertheless, we did think think
couple Number 2 shoul'dve had another go at the Lambada
when the judge was to late to see all their perfourmance.

Checking

Ask a colleague to check your copying and correcting work
(see page 75 for corrected version).

File any work in which your colleague finds error(s), after you've
marked it with a note of the cause of your mistake(s).

Retrieve your work from Working Session 32. Re-type any work if
uncorrected errors were found. If you were accurate, then re-type
the drills to try and increase your speed.

> **Corrected version – Working Session 32**
> We do not need your help (although we are grateful for the offer)
> in the matter currently outstanding. If you are able to give us
> some assistance in the future – particularly with our social work
> – we shall be pleased.

WORKING SESSION 33

Increase your working speed

Type this memo. Try to get it ready for signature within 20 minutes. Check and correct circled word 'creditted'.

(Memo)

From J Dennison

To J Baxter

You asked Sally Brickley last week to let you have figures for Midlands and Wales sales of goods in the "Abode" range. Sally has now collected the data thro' A & M Associates, but you will no doubt appreciate that their figures are produced on a different basis from the ones you require.

This is because "Abode" goods ~~are~~ may be sold thro' distributors and some orders may be (creditted) to agents who are not distributors.

However, we have now ~~provided~~ compiled the data and ~~hope~~ it wl serve your purpose:

SALES OF
ABODE RANGE (£000)

MIDLANDS

1991	1992	1993 (estimated)	Item No
228	216	200	Ab684
22	18	20	Ab433

WALES

1991	1992	1993 (est—)	Item No
14	8	5	Ab684
8	6	5	Ab433

Confirming facts

In the two previous Working Sessions, you had to fill gaps in the draft memos from information in other tasks. In offices, and in exams, people drafting in handwriting often take short-cuts and leave the typist/operator to fill in the gaps.

Type the following three letters, filling in the gaps from information readily available to you in the drafts.

Task 1

43 Linston Terrace

Fennyman Street

Sheffield S4 3LT

F D Hope Esq
Sales Director
Praciteles Group
Adam Street
London WC2N 6EZ

Dear Mr H___

My neighbour, Mr J Janison of 41 L___ T___, has recommended that I contact you for details of the nearest stockist of your product, 'Praxiwrap' Loft Insulation.
Your previous agents in this town, J & D Bix of Main Street, Sh___, have moved away.
Yours faithfully

Task 2

43 L___ T___
F___ St
Sheffield S4 3LT

Mr B. D Smithie
43 Church Lane
Bentwood
Yorkshire S9 4JD

Dear Mr Smithie
Thank you for your letter + telephone calls regarding the completion of work at my house + supply of material for loft in ___.
My neighbour, Mr Janison of 41 L _ T__, has recommended 'Praxiwrap', but I have been unable to locate the supplier. I have today written to Mr Hope, Sales Dir___ of Praxi___ G___ in London, and will contact you again when he replies.
Yours sincerely
James Johnson

WORKING SESSION 33

Spot the mistakes

Aim to type the following in three minutes, correcting all the mistakes (there are seven):

TYPE GROUP MEETING ON THURSDAY

This Group frequently recieves requests for help from
prospective pet owners in search of healthy animals.
It have therefor been sugested that we should produce
a list of suitable pets. this would include brief detais
of aminals available together with the breeder's name
and telephone number.

SAVE IT

Check and file

When you're sure you've got it right, file the above for use in the Workshop in Working Session 47. Word processor users will need to bring it back to screen.
There's a corrected version on page 154.

Setting-up

Aim to set tabs and type the following in five minutes.

TYPE

Name of event	Estimated Duration		Contact at venue
	From	To	
Art in the North	Apr	May	Rick Hayes
Costume in the Middle Ages	Oct	Dec	Jan Sellsdon
Sculpture Woprkshop	Jul	Sep	Chris Soud
Victorian Games and Toys	Jan	Feb	Jan Sellsdon

Keyboard skill

Type as fast as you can:

TYPE We were there when they decided the new, higher kitchen
ceiling needed brightening. They used fresh designs
with lighter tints. This succeeded in giving better,
brighter light.

Accurate?

Excellent, type the next exercise.

Made mistakes?

Try again, this time more slowly, and get it right before moving on.

Type as fast as you can:

TYPE They went in their new vehicle, but were very undecided
where the best scenery might be seen during the ride.

135

Task 3

43 L__ T__
F____
Sheffield S4 __

Mr T Jenkins
28 Manton Avenue
BINGLEY
Yorkshire
BY4 8SF

Dear Tom

Do you know whether 'Praxiwrap' L__ In____ is the best possible product for use in a house such as mine? My neighbour, Mr J__ of 41 L__ T__, has recommended it.

Even if it is the best, I cannot ~~trace~~ trace the local stockist, although I have written to the Sales Dir____ of the manufacturers & hope to hear soon.

If you would advise another make I would like to know. Thank you;
Best wishes

The words for the gaps were:

Task 1	**Task 2**	**Task 3**
Hope	Linston Terrace	Linston Terrace
Linston Terrace	Fennyman Street	Fennyman Street
Sheffield	insulation	S4 3LT
	Linston Terrace	Loft Insulation
	Director	Janison
	Praxiteles Group	(or J Janison)
	James Johnson	Linston Terrace
		Director

SECTION ONE

33 WORKING SESSION

Try to sort and type/print the following table in 30 minutes:

Please re-arrange events into alphabetical order within each venue.
Retain abbreviations

FORTHCOMING EVENTS

Name of event	Estimated duration		Contact at venue
	From	To	

(Leave space here at least 38 mm (1½") deep)

MERCIAN CENTRE

Jitinder Kohli

Art in the North	Apr	May	~~Rick Hayward~~
Costume in the Middle Ages	Oct	Dec	Jan Sills
Sculpture Workshop	Jul	Sep	Chris Souter
Computer Graphics	Feb	Apr	Peter Davey Jitinder Kohli
Painters of the Past	Jun	Aug	~~Rick Hayward~~
Origami Extravaganza	Mar	May	Chris Souter
Unusual Perspectives	May	Aug	Peter Davey
Victorian Games and Toys	Jan	Feb	Jan Sills

CORONATION HALL

Etchings and Engravings	Mar	May	June Hill
Looking Back at Pop Art	Jan	Apr	Bill Shaw
Machines and Inventions	May	Jul	Simon Archer
Pictures and Music	Feb	Apr	Bill Shaw
Seaside Views of the Past	Jul	Aug	Kevin Simpson
Surrealism in Retrospect	Apr	Jun	Sue Price

GREY'S ART GALLERY

Canals of Venice	Apr	May	David Riley
Victorian Narrative Paintings	Oct	Nov	Lucy Wilson
Outer Space Explored	May	Sep	Sally Jones
Art and Archaeology	Aug	Nov	Pat Calder
Portrait Photography	Jun	Aug	David Riley
Woodblock Engraving	Apr	Sep	Sally Jones
Young Artists of Britain	Jul	Aug	Pat Calder

Warm-up: Rhythms

TYPE

```
pew few sew fun run bun sun jug rug hug lug tug fug
dug saw was dot fair hair lair dare ware rare pare
bear wear pear pair care mare share where chair here
swear blair flair their Clare Clair glare church
breath grudge freeze frozen apples poplar kipper
jumper pew fair share church few hair where breath sew
lair chair grudge
```

Copying practice:
Keep your place; watch for similar lines

TYPE

It may not be possible to avoid running into
problems at first.
It may not be necessary to look on the
gloomy side of things but we all know
it is hard to make it when working alone.
Nevertheless, it is also true that we all know
there are benefits to doing so.

Punctuation: Quotation marks

TYPE

```
"How awful!" shouted Penny.  "What?" Harry bawled back.
"That lorry with the rotten fruit on it."
"If I wanted any - and I don't - I wouldn't buy fruit
from that company.  Would you?"
"Which company?" asked Harry.
"The one whose lorry is carrying rotten fruit!"
```

Spot the mistakes

Re-type the following, correcting the errors (there are seven):

TYPE

```
It is approximatly six months since your apointment as
Correspondance Officer and it will soon be necesary to
arrange for you to recieve details of payments to
which you are entitled for initiall expences.
```

Ask a colleague to check your copying and correcting work
(see page 77 for corrected version).
File your work.

Retrieve work from Working Session 33 and re-type any in which
errors were found. If you were accurate, re-type the drills and try
to increase your speed.

> ### Corrected version – Working Session 33
> It's (or it is) not for us to complain about other people's
> failures in the dance championship (their failure may improve
> our opportunities). Nevertheless, we did think couple Number 2
> should've (or should have) had another go at the Lambada when
> the judge was too late to see all their performance.

SKILLS PRACTICE

SECTION ONE

Sorting and re-arranging

This simple routine can save you time, as well as preventing your leaving out items accidentally:

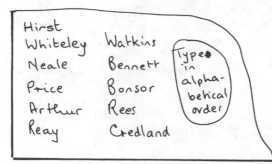

- Count items to be rearranged (eleven in the example above).
- Number items on the draft, in order of typing – as shown above.
- Check your numbering tallies with your count (eleven).
- Type, and tick each item when completed.
- Count your final typed list to make sure all (eleven) are there.

Aim to sort and type within five minutes:

Type in alphabetical order

About this Century
Hollywood and its Stars
Enigma at Large
Sherbert and Friends
Wellywig Woods
Freddy Goes Home
Birthday Blues
The Primrose Line
Larry's Cave
Garden Games

Bernie the Bear
Paper and Paste
Jerry on the Train
Service Militaire
Pierre's Lorry
Tabatha
Emily and Ginge
Oscar at the Dance
The Picnic Set

CHILDREN'S TITLES NOW IN PRODUCTION

It is common to centre text such as chapter headings or titles. This can be done automatically by word processors and electronic typewriters.

At the start of Section One, you ran a machine check which included automatic centring. You'll have your record there to remind you how to use the centring function.

Using a typewriter which will not centre automatically:

- If you have margins set, add the margin points together and divide by two; this figure is the centre of your typing line. Move your carriage along to this point.

- If you have no margins set, check the left edge of your paper is at 0 on the scale on the paper bail (the slim bar holding down your paper); then look to see the number on that scale the right edge reaches – and divide that figure by two. This figure is the centre of your paper. Move your carriage along to this point.

- Backspace once for each two letters or spaces in the title or heading. Type at that point.

- When you have more than one line to be centred, set a tab stop at the centre of your line or paper. You can then move quickly each time to the centre to start backspacing.

Type the following short notices centring each line:

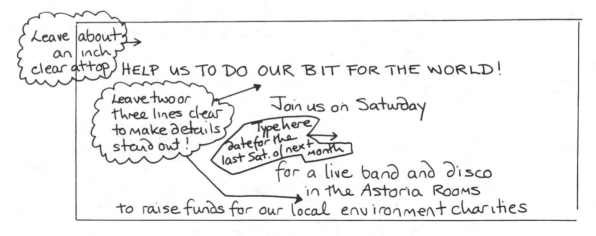

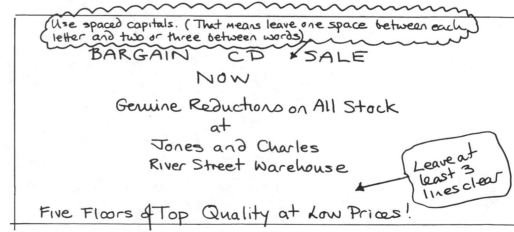

SECTION ONE

Highlighting – bold and underlining

Type the following extract and memo. If you are using a typewriter which doesn't have **bold** then in the extract use underline instead of bold.

(Extract) (Print in double linespacing please)

T H E   P O L I T I C A L   F A C T O R

You will have been aware for some time that my chapter "Fourteen Facets of Management" (BOLD) arises from my exp in the nationalised sector. Here, the hidden influence was from govt. We do not now need to be squeamish about the need to take a/c of this factor.

Within my Co, as long as we reward stakeholders, (bold) we can change – within reason – in any way we wish.

Choosing to Work (caps) (bold)

Many of our People are no longer totally dependent upon a job for the basic necessities of life. They CAN and DO choose. However, we must have a great deal of commitment, skill and enthusiasm from them (their) (with us) if we are to succeed. (bold)

(Memo)

From   J D Holmes
To   COUNTER SALES – P Phillips

DISC 0198   SERIES A10

The above disc is NOT to be supplied with orders for DRUM 6812 unless the written order specifies DISC AND DRUM 6812.

This instruction applies with immediate effect and to ALL customers (Inset this paragraph)

In the case of query contact me or Paly on Ext 162. If neither of us is available Najrit will advise (Ext 143).

Warm-up: Spacing

Leave two spaces between words here:

TYPE

```
Rattle down the railway lines
to Bow.
1990  1991  1992  1993  1994  1995  1996  1997  1998
1999  2000
Fix the hammer by putting the
head on.
```

Copying practice:
Repeating letters ending/starting words

TYPE

```
Fred didn't take enough, having great trouble earning
Gary's share.
We ended down near Rallings Street towards Savanna Avenue.
That tariff falls sharply. Our rates seem more enduring.
```

Find the right word

Use the words below to fill in the gaps:

TYPE

```
..... ideas .... not about ..... the programme was
leading, but about what ...... they could give to the
......... about its aims and ......... .  There were
... many people wanting .. ...... her.


where  to  advice  Principal  Their  were  principles
too advise
```

Timing

Aim to type the following accurately within one minute
(approximately 25 words a minute):

TYPE

There will be a members' meeting at the Leisure Club tonight. The main reason for the meeting is to consider the bill for re-tiling the showers.

Checking

Check your own timed typing, and then get a colleague to double check it. Re-type if either of you find any errors.

Don't begrudge the time and trouble to get things right.

> **Corrected version – Working Session 34**
> It is approximately six months since your appointment as Correspondence Officer and it will soon be necessary to arrange for you to receive details of payments to which you are entitled for initial expenses.

35
WORKING SESSION

Spot the mistakes

Type the following. Correct all the errors (there are fourteen).

```
Thank you very much for your telehpone call today.  We are in-
-deed glad to hear that that Dark Beauty has made such an swift
improvement after the fall sustained during excercise last week.
It is usaully the case than recovery form such a injury is
totall.  It leaves no lasting side affects.  Nevertheless, I
confirm that we will check during rouetine visits to ensure that
good progrss is maintaned.
```

Check

Ask someone to check your work with you. Make sure you found all the errors – and that you didn't make any others. There's a corrected version on page 154.

Remember: your word processor Spellchecker will not help you with several of these errors!

Highlighting

Type the following notes on highlighting. File your paper copy for easy reference.

```
HIGHLIGHTING

INSETTING
One way to highlight and
You can attract attention to a short passage ʌis by leaving extra
space clear around it -- this is called INSETTING.

Example:

        It is important for everyone that we all make quite sure

                NO MEMBER OF STAFF USES
                STAIRCASE A BETWEEN 10
                AND 11 AM TOMORROW

        Please ensure all of your staff are informed.


Use your judgement        keep all the abbreviations

You're not usually told an exact number of spaces to inset.  Take
account of:

-- the extra space needs to be enough to attract attention
-- narrow insets, eg only 3 spaces, won't make much difference
   to appearances so won't be very effective
-- 1" to 1 1/2" either side will highlight a paragraph.
        Type as 1½" if you can
Using a word processor?

Move to a tab stop to start the indent lines, and tap return at
the short line-ends.
```

Machine check

You used tabs in Working Session 12, in the Keyboard Section. We shall now include headings at the top of each column, and a general heading across the page.

Word processing packages often include a set of tab stops already in place, and it is usually possible to use these for any job with columns. You must remember, of course, to leave room for the longest line in the column. If the set tab stops really do not fit the columns you want to type, your manual will tell which keys to press and what steps to take.

Type this letter which includes a 3-column table. Use tab stops for the columns to save yourself time; remember to leave enough space for the longest line in each column.

Mr C Anderson
J Lancaster & Associates
25 Warwick Street
OXFORD
OX2 9LX

Dear Sir

Thank you for your recent enquiry. We are now able to set out below the info. you require.

CITY	DURATION OF COURSE	LEVEL
Granada	14 nights	Advanced
Cordoba	7 nights	Intermediate
Seville	21 nights	Advanced

We enclose our latest brochure wh. lists hotels and dates available. The courses are popular and early bookings are required.

If you wd. like to discuss anything in more detail, please call us on Freephone 0800 222 888 during office hours (8.30 am to 5.30 pm).

Yours faithfully
PRAXITELES GROUP

remember to include date and 'enc'

Sally Adams

WORKING SESSION 35

Type the letter and a label addressed to:

Mr M Parry
Parry Photographic Ltd
8 Bell Lane
Milton Keynes
MK3 1XY

Dear ~~Mr Parry~~ Mike

Remember the copy for Jo

Another commission has now developed and I hope you can help us again.

I have asked Jo James, our showroom manager (Aston), to telephone you this week to arrange a time when you can photograph premises, products and presentation materials. Jo will give you all the details of the project.

We wd like the work to be completed by the end of the month so that we can include prints in our spring brochure. In addition, we hope to have some ~~life~~-size versions *(full-)* for our exhibition stand. ~~Our~~ The dates of our next exhibition are ← *Give dates for Mon - Fri, second week of next month.*

Yours sincerely

Pam Pratley
General Manager

Check

Did you:

- remember to date both the letter and the memo?
- type 'Enc' or make some other note that there was another document with the memo?

When you're sure they're right, file your documents. Word processor users will not need to bring them back to screen again.

WORKSHOP 3

Warm-up: In and out

TYPE
```
a;sldkfjghfjdksla;sldkfjghfjdksla;sldkfjghfjdksla;sldk
fjghfjdksl
A;SLDKFJGHFJDKSLA;SLDKFJGHFJDKSLA;SLDKFJGHFJDKSLA;SLDKFJ
GHFJDKSL
a;sldkfjghfjdksla;sldkfjghfjdksla;sldkfjghfjdksla;sldk
fjghfjdksl
```

Copying practice: Left hand review

TYPE
```
Twelve winning horses at the Westerham Stables went into
the Winners' Enclosure. Queen Esther presented the trophies
and the twelve winning jockeys were rewarded with prizes
of Westerways Jackets and Waistcoats.
```

Spelling practice

TYPE
```
The temporary routes through the two separate areas were
recommended by the government secretaries responsible for
quaranteeing accommodation for all nominees of both committees.

There will definitely be sufficient opportunities for all
the miscellaneous matters to be referred to the respective
businesses and manufacturers. On receipt, the accounts will
be given immediate attention.
```

Timing

Aim to type the following accurately within one minute
(approximately 25 words a minute):

TYPE
```
We acknowledge that there has been inconvenience for everyone
involved whilst the major road and pavement repairs have
been taking place in Government Square.
```

Checking

Make quite sure you did not change any of the words in Spelling
Practice above.

Try again to type the Timing sentence accurately, this time within
45 seconds (approximately 30 words a minute).

Labels

Using a word processor?

If your system is set up for labels, you'll already have been preparing labels to attach to envelopes. If not, you can use a typewriter for labels or envelopes.

Using a typewriter?

Do a Machine Check. Use your machine guide to help you make sure:

- the card holders are in place to hold the label against the roller
- the paper bail is also against the roller (if you bring all its little rollers to the middle of the bail, they'll help to keep in place small items like labels).

If the labels you're using are in a strip, put the whole strip into the machine.

Margins

Be sure to leave half an inch at the top and at the left edge before starting to type.

Memo and letter

Type this memo and the letter on the next page. You'll need to refer to your files.

MEMORANDUM

To   Jo James

From   P Pratley   (Date for today)

Please set a date for Mike Parry to bring in his crew to take photographs as outlined at our last meeting. ~~should~~ It has now been agreed that he will engage models for the pictures with people. I suggested Wed, and I believe the crew will need 2-4 hours. Ring Mike this week with a couple of dates for him to choose.

A copy of my letter to him is attached.

All the best with the project!

Special marks include:

URGENT   PERSONAL   PRIVATE   BY HAND

CONFIDENTIAL   FAO MRS SMITH

FOR THE ATTENTION OF MRS SMITH

Special marks are typed at the top of documents, and envelopes, to draw special attention to them. Use capitals or underlining to give them emphasis.

When required in letters, type them above or below the address. Leave at least one line clear between the mark and the address.

In memos, type special marks before the heading if there is one, and above the message.

Type this urgent memo. Aim to complete it accurately within two minutes.

MEMORANDUM

From   J Pollock

To   M Singh

URGENT

Thanks for your note re Barrows & Hughes. Unfortunately you failed to include the completed form, although you referred to it.

If you will send it on to me, I can process their request by Friday.

Timed spelling

Try to type the following, with all words spelled in full, in no more than two minutes.

TYPE We bel. the co. wl. dev. its bus. faster when full-time staff are resp. for the a/cs. There are other misc. ways in wh. savings cd. be made immed.

Check spellings

Refer to the list of words in Section One page 65 to check your spellings.

Develop your keying speed

Type as fast as you possibly can – there are lots of double letters:

TYPE
```
Is it better to have butter for supper as well as
dinner or did you mutter that in summer you like
less fatty meals?
```

Now type the following, this time at your normal speed and without errors:

TYPE
```
It is possible that your disappointment will be assuaged
by the opportunity to call at the new offices tomorrow.
```

Retrieving work and modifying layout

Find from your paper file the list of words you typed in Working Sessions 16 and 19 in the Keyboard Section of this book.

Re-type the list:

- start with the heading WORDS AND MEANINGS
- sort the list into alphabetical order of the words, and include the word 'assuaged'
- type the list in two columns, headed 'Word' and 'Meaning'.

The start is set out for you here:

TYPE
```
WORDS AND MEANINGS

Word                          Meaning

assuaged                      softened, mitigated, allayed
```

MEMO

From   Andrew Irvine

To   Senior Management Team :

     Alphege Roberts - finance

     Gaynor Jones   - manufacturing

     James Milligan - sales and marketing

     Laxmi Chaudhry - human resources

CONFIDENTIAL

Any special mark, eg CONFIDENTIAL should be typed before the message and with a space above and below.

Redundancies

I've heard this morning that the Excelsior Hotel Group has gone into receivership. Not only ~~are they~~ *is it* of our largest debtor, ~~they~~ *it has* ~~have~~ also been our largest customer for contract carpeting.

(NP) //Domestic carpet manufacture is down 35% on last year. If we cannot replace the Excelsior capacity, contract carpeting will be down 47%. Our current short-time working will not give us enough savings on overheads. *The state of* / Our own cash flow and order book means we need to make savings rapidly.

(NP) //Please be in the board room at 7.30 am tomorrow morning. I would like suggestions on: how we might replace Excelsior work; the type of redundancy policy to implement; what this might cost in the short term; use of local out-placement company to counsel ex staff.

(NP) //Please bring your salary budgets and overhead costs for the year and latest sales projections.

Type the letter to Mr Miller. You'll need to refer to your files.

Our ref ~~AW/PE~~ ACB4/PC

Mr M Miller
~~23 Lime Rd.~~ (see below for extra details)
WARRINGTON
Cheshire
WA1 3EZ

Dr. Mr Miller

ANNUAL CHARITY BALL

Thank you for yr. letter ~~wh. arrived by hand yesterday.~~ wh. I recd. yesterday.

I am enclosing a copy of the minutes of the last cttee. meeting. These wl. answer your questions about this year's ball, which wl. be discussed at a meeting on ~~give date here from the memo you have on file~~ ✳ *(from Working Session 41)*

// The first ball did indeed take place ~~during the reign of Queen Victoria~~ in 1873. At that time, suff. money was raised to help found the cottage hospital. This building now provides temp. accom. for the college. These days, the ~~proceeds~~ funds are divided up and sent to a number of local charities. A list of these charities is in the Town Hall entrance. ~~This ensures that everybody is kept informed of where the money goes.~~ (displayed on the notice board)

We are always pleased to welcome members of the (press/local) and I will send you a special press badge in due course.

Yours scly.
P Carter
Secy.

Mr M Miller
Features Editor
Cheshire Echo
23 Lime Rd etc etc

Check

Did you spell out all words accurately including:

Road, Dear, receive, committee, sufficient, temporary, accommodation, sincerely, Secretary?

Did you remember to type 'Enc' at the foot of the letter, or to give some other reminder that something extra to the letter should be sent?

File

When your work is accurate, file your paper copy. You will not need to bring this work to screen again.

Time yourself and aim to type the following in three minutes:

In RSA exams, don't type in special marks unless you see them in the draft.

Type special marks in capitals or with initial capitals and underlining. In the exam, use the style used in the draft.

Special marks must be at the top of the document and on any envelope or label which goes with it. Separate the mark from the address or the message by at least one clear linespace.

Check

Finished in three minutes? Accurate?

You're copying at about 25 words a minute.

Made mistakes?

It's better to type more slowly and accurately. Try again more slowly, and when it's right move on.

Following instructions

Type the following as quickly as you can. Follow the instruction at the top to make corrections all through the task.

Change 'index'/indexes to 'name'/names all through

Some people find it useful to keep a written note of the indexes they give to documents.

If you use a small word processor you may have to shorten file indexes, and the index does not appear automatically on the document. It can then be quite difficult to remember what is in each file without a separate record of indexes and contents.

Note

It is quite common for writers to give only one instruction which you have to carry out several times throughout a document.

The surest way to remember is to go through the document and make all the changes on the draft before you start to type.

WORKING SESSION 37

Spelling

Type the following notes:

SPELLING

In this book, just as in an office, words appear in abbreviated form to save time for the writer. You have to ∧ type them in full. ~~to show that you~~ ⟨know their spellings so that you can⟩

// As well as the words already shortenered in this book (listed for you in Section One ~~two~~) the following may be used from now on:

altho' for although   org for organisation
poss for possible   asap for as soon as possible

Check

After checking with the list on page 65, file the above.

Type the following, spelling out all the words. Type as fast as you can.

Dear Sirs

W. ~~ref~~ to yr. letter, please reserve accom for us on 10 of next month. We need three rooms in which to hold approx 20 recruitment interviews ~~appts~~. These are a result of our recent adverts. for staff in yr. area.

We ack rec of yr a/c for last month and altho' we have one or ~~two~~ queries, we sh settle asap.

Yrs ffly

Check

Make sure your spelling is accurate, as well as your keying. If you made mistakes, try again, more slowly, so as to get it right before filing. There's a corrected version on page 154.

WORKING SESSION 42

An instruction to 'justify margins' means the text must be aligned at both left and right.

Using a word processor or an electronic typewriter with Justification function?
Look at your manual/guide to see the commands and steps you should use.

Using a typewriter with no Justification function?
Follow directions below.

Type the draft contents page.

Directions:
- type the first line in the position you want it
- set a tab stop in the next letterspace after 'Forests'
- return
- use your tab key to move to the tab stop
- backspace once for each letter and space in the next line
- type next line
- repeat the last four steps for following lines.

```
Chapter 1        Page 6        Saving the Forests
                                            Africa
                                          Malaysia
                                   Central America

Chapter 2          44           The Sea Population
                                            Whales
                                        Crustaceans

Chapter 3          62                    Our Land
                                   Northern Europe
                                  Southern Europe
                                             Asia
                                The sub-continents        caps

Chapter 4         110                     Climates
                                          Deserts
                                         Humidity
                                      Wind Speeds
```

Check

Word processor users will not need to bring this back to screen.

When you've made all your corrections, move on to Working Session 38.

House style

Some organisations like all correspondence, when produced by word processors, to have justified left and right margins. Check and follow house style. This style is not used with typewriters which do not have the justification function.

UNDERPINNING KNOWLEDGE • JUSTIFYING

Check

When you've checked, ask someone else to read the memo you've typed for Phil Carter. Did you:

- date it with today's date?
- make all the alterations accurately?
- make six paragraphs?
- type 'shall' instead of 'sh'?
- make enough copies?

Accurate first time?

File the memo for easy reference – you'll need to refer to it again.

Made mistakes?

It's worth taking the trouble to get your work accurate. Have another try. When you're sure it's right, file the memo for easy reference later on.

Tabulation

Type the following table. Practise applying an instruction, given once, throughout a piece of work:

SWITCHBOARD RELIEF ROTA

	11.30–12.30	12.15 – 1.15	1.00 – 2.00
January	*(Should be Jayne. Change all through, please)*		
Week 1	(Jane) Perriott	Maisie Blu	Fred Harper
2	Maisie Blu	Jim Sellinge	Kim Hayes
3	Kim H —	Jane Perriott	Madge Bills
4	Fred H —	Madge B —	Wayne Ford
February			
Week 1	Jane Perriott	Jim Sellinge	Fred Harper
2	Wayne Ford	Kim H —	Maisie B —
3	Karen Swift	Madge B —	Jane Perriott
4	Sandy Wells	Hilda Bache	Karen Swift

Type the article called 'Line Justification' and:

- practise copying and checking longer documents
- read and take account of the content, which is underpinning knowledge for you
- practise following one instruction throughout a document.

Using a typewriter without Justification function?
Type the article with a ragged right margin.

Using a word processor or electronic typewriter with Justification function?
Use your manual/guide to see the commands and steps you should use.

change 'justification' to 'justify' throughout

Line Justification

If you're using a word processor, use a 'justified right margin' ~~all the~~ through.

The following paragraphs ~~is~~ *are* justified with a line length of 50: *(leave one clear line)*

> Contrary to popular belief, most burglaries take place during the day. The quick dash you make to the shops before they close, or to collect the children from school, presents ideal opportunities. The tell-tale garage door left open because you did not have time to slam it shut before you rushed away, ~~as~~ *is* good as an invitation. *(leave one clear line)*

With the 'justification' function on you can type in the normal manner (with no need to press the return key at line-ends). ~~As you reach and pass the right margin, your cursor will move to the next line.~~ Extra spaces will then be spread among the typed words to fill up lines ~~without going past the~~ *to make a straight* right margin.

Some software always has the justification function on unless you turn it off, *(the 'default')*.

If you had to turn ON 'justify' to type with straight margins, then be sure to remember to turn it off when you've finished the work (or the part) you were asked to set out in this way.

SKILLS PRACTICE • JUSTIFYING

WORKING SESSION 38

SECTION ONE

Type the memo to Jane Edwards, taking the copies and routing one to Jim Woods.

(Memo)

Ref ~~AW/PC~~ ACB3/PC

From Phil Carter

To Jane Edwards

URGENT

ANNUAL CHARITY BALL

I have now booked the board room for the ~~meeting on Wednesday~~ give date for Wednesday of next week.

// Before then I sh. need to know how many tickets have been ordered from the printers. When can we expect delivery? We need to clear 300 to make a worthwhile profit. We are not allowed more than 400 because of fire regulations. // Both bands have now confirmed their bookings and background music has been arranged for the supper room. Have you made any plans for the press to be provided with food and drink? ~~There were complaints last year and we do not want to antagonise~~

Mrs Finch is dealing directly with the catering firm and they will be responsible for all china, cutlery and linen. This will lighten our work load.

One matter which has not been resolved is that of storing the raffle prizes. They will start to arrive very shortly and there is no room for them here. Please check with the staff at the Town Hall to see if they can offer to help us.

Lastly, please let me have a copy of the top table plan for the supper room. This can be passed to Mrs Finch for her views.

Copy to Jim Woods

(Copies 1 + 2)

Allocating space

Type the following, leaving exactly the amount of space shown:

We shall be holding a
*

leave 4 spaces at *

SWIMMING GALA
*

at BURNTWOOD LEISURE CENTRE
*

on Saturday next
✉

leave 2 spaces at ✉

use double line-spacing

Those taking part will be

- Fifth Form, Berryhouse School
- Brownies, Juniors and Infants, Balehouse School
- Sixth Form, Wensleyfields School
✉

In aid of Cancer Research Fund

Increasing speed

Type the following as fast as you can:

In the Inn we watched the television and saw the innings of the England cricket team in their match against the Australians. After that we strolled round to the airport and found we had to wait another two hours. We went to the television lounge, only to find the programme was a video of the same innings!

Spelling

Type the following. Spell out all the words and aim to finish within two minutes.

Following recent govt. legislation, and changes to a/c procedures for dealing w. depreciation, we are no longer happy with the way your co. is presenting our final a/cs. We wd like a senior partner to take personal resp. immed. We wd also like info on how we shd. keep our monthly depreciation a/cs.

Check

If you were accurate and finished in time, move on to the next practice.

If not, then re-type until you can type the paragraphs accurately. It's better to type more slowly than to rush and make mistakes.

SKILLS PRACTICE

WORKING SESSION 39

Post-dating

Type the following. It is information you'll need before typing the memo in the Workshop in this Session.

Time yourself: aim to finish, including checking, within ten minutes.

POST-DATING

Future dates

Keep a calendar handy to see future dates. ~~Always~~ give the actual date rather than just the day. then there's less chance of a mistake.

Keep abbreviations
You can then
when making appointments

Extra copies

In addition to a paper copy for your file, you'll *often* need an extra copy of documents. In the memo for the Workshop in Working Session 41 you are asked for '1 + 2' meaning the top copy to Jane Edwards plus one for Jim Woods and one for the file.

Photocopies, ~~repeat prints~~ *additional printouts* or carbon copies are equally acceptable, *unless there is a house rule which you must follow* ~~if~~ *in your job.*

NOTE: In RSA Word Processing exams you are not expected to print the extra copies, but only to show that one would be despatched.

Leave some lines (more than one) clear after the end of the memo and type 'Copy to Jim Woods'.

Some people still use the ~~abbreviation~~ *old symbol* 'cc' instead of 'Copy to'.

Route the copy

(not the original!)

On one of the copies, highlight the words 'Copy to Jim Woods' so that it would, in the office, get sent to him. You can highlight with a highlighting pen, a tick or a handwritten underlining.

NOTE: In RSA Word Processing exams, as you don't have to print ~~the~~ extra copies, you don't have to highlight.

Check

Read through these notes on post-dating. When you're sure they're right, file your paper copy for easy reference.

Type the article called 'Making corrections', which continues on page 87 and:

- practise copying and checking longer documents (remember – when you get bored, take a break for a second or two)
- read and take account of the content, which is underpinning knowledge for you
- practise following one instruction throughout
- allocate space as instructed.
- use A4 paper and make a page break no more than 2 inches from the bottom of the page. Check back to your Section One notes if you don't know how.

MAKING CORRECTIONS ⟨Adjust your typing line to 60⟩ ⟨number 2nd page⟩

WHEN USING A WORD PROCESSOR WITH SPELLCHECK
⟨Use capital S for Spellchecker all through⟩

Run your **S**pellchecker in every item of work. Don't forget it!

Look at your manual/guide to see the commands and steps you should use.

Your spellchecker can save you a lot of time by immediately finding any words you've typed which are not in its dictionary. Most keying errors will be found by your spellchecker because the mistakes will make words which your spellchecker can't recognise.

You will still need to correct from the screen because your spellchecker will not highlight words which are in its dictionary, and you may have used real words in error.

For instance, you might type 'advice' instead of 'advise'. The word 'advice' will be recognised and passed by the spellchecker. You would need to compare what you've keyed in with the draft before you would find this sort of mistake.

It's often better to stop and check your screen at the end of each section rather than have to read from the beginning.

WHEN USING A TYPEWRITER

Corrections should be unnoticable at first glance.

Use correcting materials gently! This is because:
⟨Leave one clear line at *⟩
- erasers can make holes or dirty marks if you scrub too hard
- paper or plastic correcting strips spread on to other letters if you hold them too firmly against the paper
- fluid leaves lumps if you use too much or don't use thinners
- lift-off tape leaves the words 'bold' if you increase the pressure to make the correction come through on a carbon copy.

Any method will be satisfactory, and will be acceptable in RSA exams, when the correct word(s) or characters are:
- not blurred or bold in contrast with your other work
- level with the other words on the same line (if you've spotted the mistake after taking the paper out of your typewriter and put it back to make the correction)

When you're using fluid, it's obviously important to let it dry thoroughly before you type the new letter or word. If you carry on typing while you wait for the fluid to dry, do remember to go back and fill the gap!

SECTION ONE

Stationery

At the back of this book there is sample stationery which you may photocopy for use throughout this book.

If you have to use plain paper, leave about 2" clear at the top for letterheads and type details for memos as you have in Section One.

Machine check

Using a word processor?

Look at your manual and run a machine check to make sure you can:

▶ use the commands to end pages as asked in drafts (Page Break)

▶ key in and set a **header** (a heading which will be automatically repeated at the top of each sheet)

▶ key in and set a **footer** (a heading which will be automatically repeated at the foot of each sheet).

Using a typewriter?

Look at your manual and check to make sure you can:

▶ find the cardholders (usually two plastic shields either side of the printing point) and check they're in place

▶ recognise the paper bail (the slim bar which holds down the paper against the roller)

▶ use the paper scale.

Qualifications

The work in this section will be useful for those people studying for RSA Stage II exams, document production in NVQ level 2 as well as elements 2.3 (Supply information for a specific purpose) and 2.4 (Draft routine business communications).

CARBON COPIES

If you can correct carbon copies at the same time as
correcting the original, so much the better. Always
protect the copy:

- hold the top copy and carbon paper forward while the
fluid dries on the copy

- slip a scrap of paper between carbon paper and copy
while you use an eraser.

If you're using lift-off correcting ribbons it's often
better to wait until you take work from the typewriter to
correct carbon copies. If you're correcting several
words, it's still better to slip a scrap of paper between
carbon paper and the copy while you make the correction on
the original. ~~The extra carbon in overtyping is more~~
~~difficult to remove or cover when you correct the copy.~~

USE A VARIETY OF METHODS

METHOD	BEST FOR
Soft pencil eraser	Carbon copies
Pencil-shaped hard eraser	Single letters
Thin fluid	Single letters
Thicker (but not lumpy)	Words
	Carbon copies
Paper/plastic correcting strips	Top copies *but not good*
Lift-off tapes	Top copies *on carbon copies*

Type bracket key on each line, ie }

Half-spacing	When two letters need
(hold down the space	to squeeze into
bar while you type)	the space for one

Check

Take time to check and correct your work.

It's sometimes difficult to concentrate to the end of a long article.

When you feel bored, make a note of where you've got to, and
have a break for a second or two before checking more.

WORKING SESSION 39

Now you're able to work on longer documents and tasks Section 2 will help you to develop your skills and increase your speed of working.

In this section each working session has a Practice Unit and a Workshop. Extra knowledge points are included, with practice in:

▶ keyboarding

▶ spelling and punctuating

▶ error-spotting

▶ setting-up (your margins, tab stops and so on)

▶ following and repeating an instruction all through a piece of work

▶ sorting items into different orders

▶ changing layouts

▶ choosing ways to highlight points in the text.

File

Open two files: one for notes from the Practice Units and another for work from Workshops.

Knowledge points are often included in the Practice Units, and you'll find it useful to be able to look back at them.

Some of the Workshop tasks have details missing, which are in the earlier Workshop items. You'll be able to find these details quickly if you keep your file handy.

Type the following article to:
- practise copying and checking longer documents
- read and take account of the contents on typing on forms.

When typing long documents it can be difficult to keep your concentration. It helps if you stop to check and correct your work after each paragraph or section.

In RSA Stage I Word Processing exams there is no pre-printed form for completion.

In RSA Stage I Typewriting Skills exams there is one pre-printed form for you to complete with information given in the question paper.

Type the following information on completing pre-printed forms.

Use a typing line of 60

USING A TYPEWRITER TO COMPLETE PRE-PRINTED FORMS

Filling in a form is a job that everyone has to do. For the typist it involves:
(*) using the machine to make sure you do not type over any of the words or lines printed on the form
(*) choosing the right information for each section.

Leave one/clear extra linespace at (*)

USING YOUR MACHINE

Interliner

Look at your machine manual/guide to find this. It's a lever, usually at the side of the carriage.

This lever frees the roller from its normal typewriting lines. You can then type between lines which are not printed the same distance apart as typewriter lines.

When you've finished the form and put the lever back into position, the roller goes back to its normal linespacing.

(cont...

Use double linespacing all through

SECTION ONE

WORKING SESSION 40

Cat. copy: <u>Hollywood Lives</u>

H—L— ⎰ Simone Marvell

sec: add bold accents in writing it necessary. Leave as 3 dots here

The ultimate exposé . . .

H—L— is a complete compendium of biographical facts about everyone who's anyone in Hollywood.

S—M— draws on her personal intimacies with the bright lights of the cinema world, ~~combined with her authorial objectivity~~ to bring you this reveªling and compelling account of Hollywood life.

(NP) [Packed with hundreds of photos, many of which ᴬ are drawn from S—M—'s personal collection and previously unpublished, H—L— brings to life in glorious ~~technicolour~~ colour both the dazzling glamour and the personal trauma of the best known ~~personalities~~ stars (✓) in Hollywood.

[What really happened behind the scenes of <u>Winter in Madrid</u>? What is Elizabeth Taylor's mystery illness? Who is Cher's secret lover?]

Learn all this and much more in H—L—, the ultimate exposé.

please emphasise in some way—inset or embolden?

Variable linespacer

Look at your machine manual/guide to find this. It's usually a small knob inside the knob used to turn the roller by hand.

You can use this knob (you push it in) to move the typewriter lines to match lines printed on the form. This method is the one to choose when the lines on the form have been printed to match typewriter linespacing.

Types of form

As well as dotted lines, many forms include boxes.

Make sure you leave some space between your typing and the lines, whichever type of ruling is on the form.

Letterheads and memo forms often have headings printed on them. You must also be sure to leave some space after headings such as 'Reference' before typing details.

CHOOSING INFORMATION

- Read through the form before you put it into the typewriter
- Look at the information you are given to type on the form
- Put a pencil cross by each item of information which has a separate heading on the form

All this is because once the form is in the machine you cannot see all of the headings. For instance, a cross by the postcode will tell you it has a separate heading so you should not type it alongside the address.

Use single linespacing for these paragraphs

One clear linespace at ✱ on this page

Check

Check your completed document carefully.

When you're sure it is right, file your work.

Word processor users won't need to bring this item back to screen.

Memo

TO: Jane Griffiths (Payroll Mgr)

From: Sheila Houston

Subject: Maria Beetley

(Mark confidential)

A salary increase of £850 has been awarded to M—B—. Her new salary will be (Sec — check my letter to M.B.). Please implement this change with effect from ~~25~~ [next month]

Please note that M—B— has also been given a promotion. Her new title is Senior Editor and this ^{and} appear on pay slips etc from now on.

On a related subject, M— has intimated to me that she would now like to join the company pension scheme. I gave Maria to understand that the current staff contribution is 4% ^{of} gross salary (am I right?). Maria wishes to ~~make~~ contribute ✓ slightly ~~greater~~ larger contributions and would like to discuss the feasibility and advisability of this with you. Could you spare her a few minutes? She'll be in contact.

SECTION ONE

- Detach the blank interview form at the back of this book (page 208).
- You should photocopy this because you will need two extra copies for the following exercise.
- Type three forms, using the information given below.

Date all forms with the
date on which you type them.

Expenses will be paid ONLY for Miss Forster

Form 1   To Miss J Forster
                    14 Blakeby Road
                    Finchleydale
                    DONCASTER DN7 8CX
Post - Administrative Officer
Contact - Mrs Margaret Woods on Extension 4406
Dates 12 - 14 February   Office: Wood Lane
                                    Easton
Times - 10 am - 4 pm

Form 2
To Mr G Barker 29 Joskin Street Menston Park
                    SHEFFIELD 9 am - 5 pm S66 9BD
Contact - Mandy Gratnor on 0302-778 4219 Ext 68
Post - Clerk at Manston Park Office

3 - 7 March   Mill Lane
3 - 4 March   Sheffield   10 am - 4 pm
                    Pond Square
                    Sheffield

Form 3
To Miss V Trippe 72 Cawood Street Angelways
                    SHEFFIELD S61 3XF
Post - Clerk at Menston Park Office
Contact - Jayne Sildon on same number as
                    Form 2, Ext 67
All other details as Form 2.

Assignment 6

In this assignment you are working for Mondori Publishing. Here you are required to type a letter and memo from Sheila Houston, the publisher, and the catalogue copy referred to in Keyboard Section, Assignment 5.

Maria Beefley
16 Field Road
~~Nottingham~~
Nottingham N12 7EY

(Mark private + confidential)

Dr M _____

Further to our conversation this ~~afternoon~~ morning I am delighted to confirm your promotion from Assistant Editor to Senior Editor.

The Comp. is also pleased to offer you a corresponding pay ~~increment~~ increase to go with yr new position. Yr annual ~~salary~~ pay ✓ wl be ~~increased~~ raised from £14,000 to £14,850. This will take affect from [sec-work out day] 30 [next month] 19__ and will represent a percentage increase of 6%. [~~May~~ I would like to] I take this opp. to thank you for all yr hard work over the past year – I know yr continued support is guteed!

Yrs scly

Sheila Houston

Publisher

cc: Perminder Rahima (Editorial ~~Manager~~ Director)

PRAXITELES GROUP

A fictitious organisation for RSA examination purposes only

Progress House   Westwood Way   Coventry CV4 8HS   Telephone 0203 470033

Our ref: ..../.......

Your ref: ..../.......

Current date

Ms Mandy Kharma
706 Twenbar Street
BIRMINGHAM
B21 4XT

Dear Ms Kharma

VACANCY FOR JUNIOR SECRETARY

Yours sincerely
PRAXITELES GROUP

Don Jakes
Sales Manager

Enc

Style guide for letters

The letter style will probably be decided by the organisation for which you work. If not, then you can choose a favourite style. In either case, the same style should be used on all letters to develop the utmost production speed.

The sample above is a basic style which you can follow. It is fully blocked (everything starts on the left) with open punctuation (no punctuation in the inside address or salutation or complimentary close).

In the meantime, shorter or longer letters can be adjusted to fit the page by varying the linespaces left clear before the reference(s), date or address; or the amount of space left for the signature area. Alternatively, you can vary the width of the left and right margins.

Sec: Type the invites - do one for each date (15, 16, 17, 18, 19 Feb) Type 2 to each A4 page

spaced caps, bold or underlined

THE ESCADIA FASHION GROUP

1 line space →

is proud to announce the showing of this year's summer collection.

2 line spaces →

. — . — . — . — . . . . . .

Sec: make a single-line decoration to write on.

2 line spaces →

is cordially invited to attend on:

1 line space →

15 february 199 — } Bold or underlined

1 line space →

at:

1 line space →

Escadia Fashion Group Showroom } Bold or u/lined

21 Bath Square

London

NC12 6IU

2 line spaces →

R·S·V·P
Rose Alphonse
Marketing Manager

Type each line from left margin

MEMORANDUM

To   M A Jones

From   J Smith

Current date

APPLICATIONS FOR JUNIOR SECRETARY POST

_____
_____
_____
_____

_____
_____
_____
_____
_____

1 _____

2 _____

3 _____

4 _____

_____
_____

Encs

Style guide for memos

The sample above is a basic style you can follow until you are in an organisation, where a standard format is usually used.

Because memos are notes between individuals in the same organisation, the formal signature area is not necessary. The sender usually adds his or her initials at the foot of the message.

Janice Wilks
Senior Buyer
Virago Fashion Head Office
12 Bedford Road
Rugby
Warks
CV13 2PE

Dr J

Thank you for coming into the office last week. It was good to meet you and finally be able to put a face to a name.

At our meeting we discussed the possibility of ~~Virago~~ Virago (✓) Fashion having exclusive rights to sell this season's new jodhpur design in polyester and rayon. As I mentioned at that meeting, we have had interest in this style from several other retailers, including one other chain store.

We therefore feel that we cannot agree to give you sole trading rights in this product unless you make a larger stock commitment. We ~~feel~~ (are of the opinion) that, given the number of outlets you have and the ~~wideness~~ size of your market, it is not unreasonable to demand a minimum initial order of 1500 garments. If you increase yr. order to this number, we can offer you an extra 1.5 ~~%~~ per cent discount.

I do hope you find this suggestion acceptable and I look forward to hearing from you soon.

Yours sncly

Robert Meecham
Sales Manager

There are a lot of companies which, these days, do not have
the computer facilities to carry out all of their own data
processing, because they prefer to use the services of a
computer bureau.

A bureau can build up sufficient custom to justify the purchase
of larger and more expensive machines than an individual
company may be able to install. This, of course, enables
the bureau to complete its work very quickly, as well as
undertaking jobs requiring very sophisticated programs and
hardware.

When we discuss the matter of the new contract at our meeting
tomorrow we must make sure Clauses 17 and 19 do not take
up too much time. Clause 21 is concerned with the individual
office worker's access to further training and must therefore
be decided upon at tomorrow's meeting.

Everything in the contract is significant in some respect,
but as next week's staff council meeting is on the subject
of training it will be more than useful to have a decision
from officers on Clause 21.

The Links
27 Marlowe Crescent
BLACKHEATH
London
SE3 6BT

Date of typing

Mr M Keane
The Watch House
19 Rangefield Drive
MILTON KEYNES
MK12 9PR

Dear Martin

I was very pleased to receive your letter. The delay in
replying is because I was away on a business trip to Holland.

Lucy and I are glad to hear that you are now quite settled
in your new home. It is not always easy to find suitable
accommodation at short notice.

The company has renewed my contract for a further period
of two years. We are very happy to know that we are definitely
settled here for that period of time.

We have made our spare room into an office. Lucy is acting
as my secretary as most of my work is now done at home. We
shall look forward to seeing you again soon.

Yours sincerely

David

Assignment 5

In this assignment you are again working for Escadia Fashion Ltd. You are asked to type an internal memo from Karen Dallas, the company director, to three members of staff. You are also to do a letter from the sales manager, Robert Meecham and an invitation, of which you must do five slightly different versions.

MEMO

To : Rose Alphonse (Marketing Manager)
Robert Meecham (Sales Manager)
Vivien Peters (Designer)

From: Karen Dallas (Director) ✓

It has been decided to exhibit selected garments from our summer collection at this yr's Yamamoti Fashion Fair in Tokyo. [Although in the past we haven't considered this show of sufficient international prominence to justify our attendance, we've recently become convinced of its growing significant in the fashion world. We therefore plan to show the highlights of our new range. These will include :

Description | Ref. no
Sequined body | 307 049 -
Sleeveless drape dress | 288 689 -
Plunging side - slit evening | 110 329 -
Split chiffon shirt | 183 099 -
Opaque slip with see-through sleeves | 092 129 -
Button - through tweed shirt | 231 089 -

[Please make the necy preparations for this show which takes place from the 8th - 11th April. Steven and I will be going to Japan a week in beforehand so wl make independent travel arrangements.

(margin note: sec: add days for these dates)

FRANCHISING

If you are thinking of going into franchising, do <u>not</u> make a hasty decision. Stop and think. Check thoroughly first. Ensure that you get the right guidance.

The buyer of a franchise buys the rights to a whole business package. A lump sum must be paid, plus a franchise fee, plus royalties.

The seller provides a famous name and its reputation. Also included in the package is the product or service, plus the know-how to ensure the success of the new outlet. There is no need for the franchisee to be an expert in the particular business chosen. You simply hire the necessary experienced staff.

To be successful you need resources, both financial and personal. You must have ambition and be prepared to work hard.

You should check the data about any offer and the track record of the company selling the franchise.

Over the next few years it is expected that the annual turnover of franchises will be more than doubled.

WORKED EXAMPLE

SECTION ONE

Word processor users
For this advertising material, you can recall work you saved
(Ref A1, page 95).

NEW CAREER OPPORTUNITIES

~~Trainee~~ Staff Vacancies ← (capitals)

Our company spends much time and effort on ~~market research. We~~ *selecting the right candidate for the right job.*
~~hope this improves the services we offer.~~

We are now looking for the right ~~people~~ *person* to ~~join our sales team.~~ *become our office secretary.*
~~However, we only recruit the best.~~

If you think you possess an ~~irresistible~~ *unflappable* personality, ~~a~~ good
~~sense of humour~~ and are not afraid of hard work, then this could
be the job for you. In return we offer a pension scheme, annual
bonus and other incentives. ~~Experience is not required as an
intensive training programme is given.~~

organizational skills

Janice Charles
Telephone ~~Mark Turner~~ for more details.

*You will need either two years' experience
on the job or an NVQ (or equivalent) qualification* (level 2)
*in Business Administration. You will also
be required to have a good knowledge
of WordPerfect 5.1 or a similar
software.*

*or ~~write~~ apply in writing, enclosing
your CV, to Mark Turner (Personnel
Manager).*

Don't rest on your laurels

Whenever you strike problems with keying, spotting errors or punctuation use the Error Clinic on pages 201-7.

To end Section One, here are some work assignments to test your skills. They are good practice for RSA Stage I exams and Unit 3 in NVQ Business Administration.

Word processor users only

These are details you will need for some of the following assignments.

- Key in the details.
- Do not print these details now.
- Save and give file names or references to suit your system.
- Assignments will include the references shown here to tell you which details are needed from your files.

Ref A1

NEW CAREER OPPORTUNITIES

Trainee Staff Vacancies

Our company spends much time and effort on market research. We hope this improves the services we offer.

We are now looking for the right people to join our sales team. However, we only recruit the best.

// If you think you possess an irresistible personality, good sense of humour and are not afraid of hard work, then this could be the job for you. In return we offer a pension scheme, annual bonus and other incentives. Experience is not required as an intensive training programme is given.

(Leave 6 linespaces clear there)

Telephone Mark Turner for more details.

Ref A2

Dear Sir (No need to justify right margin.)

Thank you for your recent enquiry. We are now able to set out below the information you require.

// We hope you will find this useful.

// If you would like to discuss anything in more detail, please call us on Freephone 0800 222 888 during office hours.

Yours faithfully

Ref A3

(Correct the circled words)

As (an) valued client we would like you to know that we are (alway) looking for ways of adding to the service we provide.

We employ staff (too) carry out market research(.) They spend much time on analysing the results. It is always most useful therefore to (recieve) your suggestions.

Typewriter users

You need not carry out this initial preparation. You will be able to type directly from the drafts when you reach the relevant assignments.

SAILING HOLIDAYS   for yachtsmen

double linespacing for this paragraph

The south coast of England offers some splendid cruising grounds.
In former years it was necy. to build castles as coastal defences
~~to protect ourselves from Spanish attack.~~ to keep enemy ships away. Today we are building
modern marinas all along the coast. This is to entice bus.
from across the Channel. At least the many foreign yachtsmen
sailing here today are more friendly!

We bel. that from Apr. to Sept. we can help you to enjoy a
summer holiday in this country. We admit we cannot
⊘ always gntee. good ~~sunshine~~ weather. ~~but there are numerous~~
~~sheltered moorings, quiet beaches and pleasant harbours.~~
Our co. has tried hard though to provide the kind of
facilities you wd. want in a modern marina.

create employment for many people to

We needed to / compete w. the marinas wh. are found
abroad.

inset this section by 6 spaces from the left margin

We offer cheaper berthing rates for yachts.

There are no hidden extras.

Our standards of service and care are first-class.
Any repair work is carried out immed. and competently
without fuss.

~~Great care has been taken in choosing staff of the~~
~~highest calibre.~~

Charter boats are well maintained. They are spacious
and fully equipped.
                    facilities you would expect ashore
All the ~~essential facilities which are so necessary~~ are
there — fuel, showers, launderette, shop, chandlery,
cafe etc.

In some quarters yachting is thought to be a sport for
the rich and elite. We have tried to dispel such an
idea. Boating is a sport which appeals to all ages
                                                    wl.
and backgrounds. We think our marinas ~~std.~~ allow
more people to enjoy the sport.

113   SECTION ONE

ASSIGNMENT 4

Assignment 1

This is an in-tray exercise. You are producing work for Lisa Menzies, exhibitions organiser for Greenery Ltd, an environmental garden product firm with a subsidiary which plans and landscapes gardens and open spaces.

The work here is:

- a draft flyer (advertising leaflet).
- a letter to a designer who is preparing some exhibition panels
- a memo to a colleague who is drafting a leaflet

You should aim to type the three items within one hour.

 G R E E N   W O R L D

GREENERY LTD

Stand No C92

Greenery Ltd was established in 1989 to produce and market environmentally - friendly products for your garden, including:

- SPRAYS FOR ~~INSECTS~~ PEST AND WEED CONTROL
- PLANT FOODS
- CLEANING MATERIALS

In 1991, we expanded. Come and see examples of what we can ~~do~~ achieve!

and we now provide a comprehensive LANDSCAPING SERVICE.

SECTION ONE

Word processor users
For this draft notice, you can recall work you saved
(Ref A3, page 95).

As ~~an~~ valued client ~~we would like you to~~ *you will* know that we are always looking

for ways of adding to the service we provide.

We employ staff ~~to~~ carry out market research, *and* ~~T~~hey spend much time on

analysing the results. It is always most useful therefore to recieve your

suggestions.

> Recall to screen, or re-type the above, + correcting as shown. Add the following. Change to single linespacing throughout. Thanks.

Our latest range of textbooks and cassettes
has ~~have~~ been produced by experts and the authors
have tried to act upon your comments. They have
provided tasks ~~that~~ give a useful, lively insight into
everyday life in Spain.

There are three books, *with* ~~and~~ accompanying cassettes wh.
have been recorded by fluent linguists'.

The text of each book are in Spanish and takes
account of all recent developments in language teaching.

One of the most successful results of our mkt. research
have been our series of language and culture learning

materials .

letter to

Stuart Diamond
Straight Line Design
Garden Warehouse
Covent Garden
London
WC2A 1LL

Envelope or label required

Dear Stuart

Thank you for sending the proposed design for our display panels for the Green World exhibition.

I'm very pleased with them overall, but wonder whether the colour scheme you suggest is a bit muted for the American market?

Please give me a call and we can discuss in more detail.

Yours sincerely

Lisa Menzies
Exhibitions Manager

Some of my colleagues are also asking if we need headings and general presentation to be more sharply focused on the market we're hoping to attract.

Mr/F Taylor (S inserted above Mr)
Larchfield
Beech Crescent EXETER
          Devon EX1 6RS

Dear Sir (Madam inserted above Sir)

                    ⌐SAILING HOLIDAYS

Thank you for your recent enquiry. We are now able
to set out below the information you require.
⟨ ✳ Insert A below ⟩
// We hope you will find this useful. ◄

// If you would like to discuss anything in more detail,
please call us on Freephone 0800 222 888 during
office hours.

Yours faithfully

✳ A Type of Yacht   Number of berths   Price per week

     Contest 41   8/9   £1.015
     Storm 33   7   £ 532
     Salter   6   £465 ~~£465~~
                                               £465

If you book your sailing holiday within
the next 2 weeks, we can offer you
a 10% discount. We enclose a
booking form.

Memo to

Liz

Lisa

LEAFLET, GREEN WORLD CONFERENCE

Stuart Diamond has produced display panel designs, which are in my office if you want to take a look.

Please finalise the leaflet copy and the wording for each of the four panels and fax it to Straight Line <u>by Monday</u>.

I'm back in the office on Wednesday. Can we meet at 11 o'clock? At that time I'd also like to talk to you and Mike about the handouts and publicity materials we ~~expect to~~ intend to use. and have in reserve Suggestions so far have been:

Day	Small flyers	Contact cards	Garden guides
1	5 000	500	200
2	2 000	200	150
3	2 000	200	150
4	3 000	200	150

Is this reasonable? We shall need to ~~prepare~~ firm up our orders by Friday at the latest.

The draft for the catalogue entry is attached. Let me know what you think as I'll have to fax the final version to the exhibition organisers by the end of Wednesday.

SECTION ONE

Assignment 4

The work is for Praxiteles Holidays – see also details for Assignment 2.

The work is:
- draft notice about the second phase of the Marina*
- letter to Mrs Taylor*
- draft advertisement for language textbooks and cassettes*
- draft advertising material for sailing holidays
- revised draft advertisement for staff*.

*Word processor users may use work previously stored (Ref A1-2-3 page 95).

Word processor users should expect to take one and a quarter hours if using recalled text.

Typewriter users should expect to take one hour and three-quarters.

Word processor users
For this draft notice you can recall the work you saved (Ref A3 page 95).

As (an) valued client we would like you to know that we are (alway) looking for ways of adding to the service we provide.

We employ staff (too) carry out market research(.) They spend much time on analysing the results. It is always most useful therefore to (recieve) your suggestions.

Our staff noted all your comments when you first viewed our waterside homes. It appears that you wanted ~~your own private~~ a club for (member's). ~~your club.~~

We are pleased to announce that we have started building the second phase of our Marina ahead of schedule. This contains a clubhouse on the northern (sides) of the harbour. It will be the ideal venue to meet friends. You can enjoy a seafood meal on the veranda while absorbing the peaceful views of the harbour.

Assignment 2

The work is for Praxiteles Holidays. This company specialises in activity holidays and has particular interests in yachting and in language courses. The assignment is typical of the work in a small firm where there are few separate departments. In such companies a secretary may do text processing for a variety of purposes.

The work is:

- letter to Mr Anderson*
- draft advertising material for Spanish holiday/course
- draft advertisement for staff*.

*Word processor users may use work previously stored (Ref A1 and A2). See page 95. Keep on file for further use.

If you are using a typewriter, or for any other reason have not typed/stored that initial work, you should type directly from the drafts which follow.

You need:

- one Praxiteles letterhead (or A4 plain paper)
- two or three sheets A4 plain paper.

Word processor users should expect to take no more than one hour if using recalled text.

Typewriter users should expect to take no more than one and a half hours.

BOOKING FORM

(Type these details on a blank Booking Form)

Please reserve a room for __42__ people. The room will be needed

on __3 February__ at __0900 hrs.__

Please complete the following:

REQUIREMENTS	QUANTITY	TIME
Morning coffee and biscuits	40 coffees 2 teas	1030 hrs
Buffet lunch	42	1300 hrs
Afternoon tea	42 with pastries	1630 hrs

(Keep all abbreviations)

Are there any special requirements   *Yes/~~No~~
(* Delete as applicable)

If Yes, please state requirements in the box provided

Lunch – white wine including 4 bottles of alcohol-free.

From __Amanda West, Publicity__   Ext __412__

Dear Sir / IMPROVE YOUR SPANISH

Thank you for your recent enquiry. We are now able to set out below the information you require.

We hope you will find this useful.

If you would like to discuss anything in more detail, please call us on Freephone 0800 222 888 during office hours.

Yours faithfully

CITY	DURATION OF COURSE	LEVEL
Granada	14 nights	Advanced
Cordoba	7 nights	Intermediate
Seville	21 nights	Advanced

We enclose our latest brochure which lists hotels and dates available. The courses are popular and early booking is required to avoid disappointment.

Address letter to:

Mr C Anderson
J Lancaster & Associates
25 Warwick Street
OXFORD   OX2 9LX

Mark it: PERSONAL

ASSIGNMENT 2

SECTION ONE

Please re-type, correcting the words that are circled. Use A4 paper and type in double linespacing, except where otherwise instructed.

BUSINESS PARTNERS MERIT AWARDS

A large volume of our sales (are) passing through third party channels. As a result, ~~this means~~ ~~that~~ our (businesss) partners are responsible for ~~the way~~ ~~how~~ our products are perceived. It is, of course, vital that a correct image is put forward. ~~forward.~~ The aim of the merit (awards') is to ask our partners to look closely at the success of their own organisations. This will enable them to discover (way) of improving customer satisfaction. This will in turn improve our image.

(the) criteria for the (merrit) awards are given below.

Inset numbered items Vacances and type in single linespacing.

1) A steady growth rate will be ~~desired~~ *required* judged by products sold against set targets.

2) The extent of staff training, response (tiem) to (customers) calls and use of the support team will be assessed.

3) Key financial statements eg stock (turnnover) will also be assessed.

Awards will be given for the best (overal) dealer, distributor, sales and marketing partners. Judging will be carried out by an independent third party. Awards will be made in (th) autumn.

ASSIGNMENT 3

Please ~~key in~~ type/print the details below in single line spacing. ~~Save under different name. Print one copy.~~ use ~~choose~~ either a ragged or justified right margin.

IMPROVE YOUR SPANISH

What better way is there of improving a foreign language than to combine lessons w. a visit to a charming city? [A team of Spanish trained teachers provides a relaxed atmosphere in wh. you will find it easy to study. They have many yrs. of exp. in teaching foreign students. You will also be given the opp. to learn more about the ~~Spanish people and their culture.~~ way of life in Spain.

on arrival

inset this paragraph by 12 spaces from the left margin only.

Following a brief 'test', students are placed in small groups. These are graded on levels of ability. Class time is then divided. Part of the time is used to dev. good grammatical habits. The rest is used to practise the oral and written language skills ~~which are necessary for complete fluency~~ you have managed to acquire during the lessons.

✓ There is a small but fully equipped library. You will Only be allowed to ~~communicate~~ ~~converse~~ in Spanish, both in class and during your leisure time. Therefore we hope that during your stay you wl. be totally immersed in the language and culture.

During free times, visits are arranged to all the 'sights'. ~~not just the historic buildings but the typical alleys and side streets.~~ each morning from 9.30 am to 12.30 pm

please key in this paragraph in double linespacing

The course includes a welcome party to meet yr. fellow students. You rec. 3 hours of tuition. You may borrow any of the exercises ~~ex.~~ and text books offered thro' the library. ~~complemented by such teaching aids as videos, computers and language laboratories.~~

A teacher is always nearby for students to consult shd. a specific language problem occur.

SECTION ONE

> Use A5 paper with the shorter edge at the top.

OUTLINE PROGRAMME

The following table gives a brief outline of the programme for the management forum "Managing Change".

TIME	ACTIVITY	ROOM
0830	Coffee on arrival	Reception area
0900	Talk "Gearing for Change" by Tony Sears	Falcon
1030	Coffee and biscuits	~~Ditto~~ Falcon
1100	Tutorial seminars	To be advised
1300	Lunch	Falcon
1430	Tutorials reconvene	To be advised
1630	Tea and pastries	Falcon
1700	Talk "Accelerating change" by Alan Peters	Kestrel
1800	Feedback session	~~Ditto~~ Kestrel
1815	Close	
1930	Gala dinner	The Royal Hotel
2015	Cocktails	The ~~Ditto~~ Royal Hotel

Seating arrangements, tutorial groups and names of leaders will be ~~advised~~ given on the day. Formal dress will be required for the Gala dinner.

Word processor users

For this advertisement, you can recall work you saved (Ref A1, page 95).

NEW CAREER OPPORTUNITIES ← (centre)

<u>Trainee Staff Vacancies</u> ← spaced capitals

Our company spends much time and effort ~~on market research.~~ discovering clients' needs. We hope this improves the services we offer.

~~We are now looking for the right people to join our sales team. However, we only recruit the best.~~

If you ~~think you possess~~ have an irresistible personality and a good sense of humour, and are not afraid of hard work, then this could be the job for you. ~~In return we offer a pension scheme, annual bonus and other incentives.~~ Experience is not required as ~~an~~ intensive training ~~programme~~ is given.

leave only 1 linespace here

Telephone Mark Turner for more details ← (capitals)

<u>Praxiteles Language Holidays</u>

We require 4 young people to assist our staff in France and Spain. You need to have a good knowledge of the 2 languages. French and Spanish The posts will suit students who are waiting to go to College and wish to earn some money.

Praxiteles L——— H——— provides the environment people want ~~in order~~ to combine a holiday with learning a language. It will be your job to assist in leisure pursuits and educational visits.

SECTION ONE

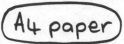
(A4 paper)

An

INVITATION ← (spaced capitals)

to join

The Praxiteles Business Partners Scheme

↕ (Leave 10 clear linespaces)

The aim ← (capitals)

The Praxiteles B____ P____ Scheme has been set up to forge stronger links between Praxiteles Group and its business partners.

The gains are many.

- An option to join an advisory council.
- Invitations to take part in a series of management forums.
- The chance to work for merit awards.

The Group will donate 25% towards all costs.

Ring us now for a free information pack. Ask for Steve Haigh or Amanda West on 0203 470033, extension 41.

Don't delay, join us in this exciting new scheme today!

SECTION ONE

Assignment 3

The work is for Peter Nolan, Sales Manager at Praxiteles Enterprises Ltd.

This is a company which runs
- training courses
- exhibitions, craft fairs and art shows
- advertising campaigns

for other companies which are members of a Business Partners Scheme run by Praxiteles Enterprises Ltd.

The work is:
- a letter and a memo about Mr Nolan's new car
- details for a new advertisement for the Business Partners Scheme
- outline programme for a management forum
- draft details of the Merit Awards Scheme
- booking form for a training day.

You need:
- Praxiteles Group letterhead, 1 envelope (or label), 1 memo form
- 1 sheet plain A5 (half A4, size approx 8.25" x 5")
- 3 sheets plain A4 (inc 1 for carbon or photocopy of letter)
- 1 blank booking form (provided at the end of this book).

You should expect to take no more than two hours.

MEMO

From Peter Nolan, Sales Manager   Ref PN/CF
To Vera Hanson, Car Fleet

I enclose a copy of a letter I have written to Charles Brookes, Managing Director of Vixen Cars.

The situation is unsatisfactory. ~~I have spoken to my dealer on the matter.~~ The new model is due to be launched in 2 months' time. I find it hard to bel. that ~~pricing~~ costing details have not yet been worked out.

Thank you for your concern. I am afraid that I cannot accept your kind offer of a spare pool car. I tow a caravan and this wd. involve me in a lot of ~~exp.~~ fitting a towbar to a temp. and then to a new car. expense

a shame
It is ~~typical of this company's bureaucracy~~ that I cannot delay ordering my new car. However, I do understand that procedures must be followed. The way forward is to hope that Mr Brookes will respond w. a price. Otherwise, I intend to submit an order for the old model. It may be that ~~in 6 months' time~~ stocks of the old model will be used up, if I leave it ~~too~~ long enough.

Thank you again for your help.

Our ref PN/CF

URGENT

Mr C Brookes
Vixen Cars
Brentford Park
COVENTRY
CV5 3QX

Please take 1 carbon copy (or photocopy)

NEW MODEL - VIXEN 700 SERIES

Dr. Mr Brookes

I am at present a driver of a 700 series Vixen saloon wh. is leased from Star Leasing plc. My company's policy is to ~~ensure that replacement vehicles are selected~~ order all new cars 3 months before the lease expires. I would very much like to select the new model of the Vixen 700 series. Sadly, Star Leasing are unable to quote a leasing price because details of the new model are not ready. As a result, the car cannot be ordered.

I am writing to ask whether you could please bring "pressure to bear" on your Fleet Sales Section to work out an approx. price. This would prevent me from having to consider choosing a car from another mfr. and from you loosing a def. sale. ~~It is never easy to win back a lost customer~~ [Please ~~could~~ let me have yourreply by the end of next week.

Yrs sncly
PRAXITELES ENTERPRISES ~~████~~ PLC

Peter Nolan
Sales Manager

Please type an envelope, or label

_____19_____

┌─────────────────────────────────┐
│ To   │
│   │
│   │
│   │
│   │
│   │
└─────────────────────────────────┘

Thank you for your application form for the post of _____

Please contact _____ on _____
to arrange an interview date.

As you probably know, we have a number of offices in your area. Interviews are being held at the following office on the days and times shown. (Please arrange your interview in accordance with the below information.)

Date(s)	Office(s)	Time(s)

Travel expenses will/will not* be paid.

* Delete as applicable

BOOKING FORM

_____ 19 _____

Please reserve a room for _____ people. The room will be needed

on _____ at _____ .

Please complete the following:

REQUIREMENTS	QUANTITY	TIME
Morning coffee and biscuits		
Buffet lunch		
Afternoon tea		

Are there any special requirements   Yes/No*
(*Delete as applicable)

If Yes, please state requirements in the box provided

```

```

From _____ Ext _____

REMITTANCE ADVICE

_____ 19 _____

To

We have pleasure in enclosing our cheque for the sum of £ _____

in settlement of the following accounts.

Your reference/ Invoice number*	Amount	Remarks
TOTAL		

Department _____

* Delete as applicable

BlottCo Ltd

24 Beaumont Street
Glasgow
GG13 7EY

GREENERY LTD
7A Pilger St, Taunton, Somerset, SA17 8HH

Escadia Fashion Group Ltd

198 Shilton St, Covent Garden, London WC2F 4BC

MONDORI

Mondori Publishing Limited, Balley Court,
Nottingham, N14 8EH

PRAXITELES GROUP

A fictitious organisation for RSA examination purposes only

Progress House   Westwood Way   Coventry CV4 8HS   Telephone 0203 470033